Dave Evans
1980

THE
SHORT WAY
TO
LOWER SCORING

THE
SHORT WAY
TO
LOWER SCORING

by PAUL RUNYAN

with Dick Aultman
Foreword by U.S. Open winner GENE LITTLER
Illustrations by Anthony Ravielli

A Golf Digest Book

Published by Golf Digest, Inc , A New York Times Company
495 Westport Avenue
Norwalk, Connecticut 06856

Trade book distribution by Simon and Schuster
A Division of Gulf & Western Corporation
New York, New York 10020

Second Printing
ISBN: 0-914178-27-X
Library of Congress: 79-52549
Manufactured in the United States of America

FOREWORD

Paul Runyan was sprinting when he first met his wife-to-be, the petite and lovely Joan Harris. He was rushing from his pro shop at the Concordia Country Club in Hot Springs, Ark., to take a phone call in the clubhouse.

As he dashed through the clubhouse door at full speed, he ran into poor Joan—face-on—and knocked her flat.

That led to a wonderful marriage that has lasted almost 50 years.

When I met Paul, about 25 years later, he was still running. He came to the La Jolla (Calif.) Country Club in the mid-1950's, when I was just starting out on the pro tour. There I practiced almost every day when I wasn't away competing. There I watched in awe as Paul dashed back and forth from his pro shop to the lesson tee. His enthusiasm seemed boundless. It infected the members at the club. It encouraged them to learn, to practice, to develop their golfing skills.

Paul affected me the same way. I played many rounds with him, and he showed me shots from around the green I had never dreamed were possible. I watched, listened and learned.

I adopted his wrist-free chipping stroke, which all but eliminates backspin from the ball. It has served me well. So have his theories on club selection, his approach to bunker play, and much, much more that he talks about in this book.

I never attained Paul's short-game proficiency. I doubt that anyone has, or ever will. The man is a genius.

But he has helped me tremendously—just as I'm sure he will help you, if you pay close attention to what he says and practice his techniques.

Today, at 71, Paul is still as enthusiastic as ever about golf, and about life in general. His lesson schedule is still fully booked at the Green Gables Country Club in Denver. He still runs to and from the pro shop. He still searches for new ways to improve his own skill and that of his pupils.

I think Paul will knock you over with this book, just as he leveled Joan Harris some 50 years ago. Then I hope you'll pick yourself up and head for the practice green to apply his methods, just as I did.

If that happens, I'm quite sure that your life will be enriched by Paul Runyan, just as Joan's and mine and thousands of others' have been.

Gene Littler
June, 1979

CONTENTS

INTRODUCTION

This is a book born of necessity, a necessity that I first realized in 1921 as a small, but eager, 13-year-old caddie at the Hot Springs (Ark.) Golf and Country Club.

That year I made two decisions. The first was that golf would be my profession. I was enamored with the game. I also liked the money. I could earn 35 cents a half hour shagging balls while Mr. Jimmy Norton, the resident professional, gave his lessons. I'd field the balls with my catcher's mitt to save a few steps. Sometimes I'd get tipped up to 50 cents. Then I'd really do a nip-up. Big money, indeed.

My second decision came about because of two brothers who were among my associates in the caddie pen. The Vanoys were strong, sturdy farm boys. Both hit their full shots far past my best efforts. I soon realized that to succeed against the Vanoys, I would need to be extremely clever on the less-than-full shots—the "part shots."

Thus through necessity, I began my lifelong devotion to the short game, the searching for shortcuts that would somehow let me compete, and hopefully excel, in a world of stronger players.

The shortcuts that I discovered and applied, though often quite radical, have served me well. I look forward to sharing them with you in this book.

If you do not drive the ball as far as your peers, I know that an improved short game can offset that deficiency. If you already have good length, I know that you can move even further up in class through better proficiency around and on the greens.

To underline what an excellent short game can do for you, I feel that here I must put myself into the uncomfortable position of talking for a moment about my career as a professional golfer.

I believe I am the shortest-hitting professional in the history of American golf who managed to be moderately successful. I say this, again, to stress the importance of the short game in one's success.

During the height of my playing days, in the 1930's and 1940's, my drives were at least 20 to 25 yards shorter than the average of the professionals then playing the PGA tour. In the tournaments and contests where our drives were measured, my average was 231 yards.

Improve Your Short Game, Lower Your Scores

This chart shows the number of strokes you can cut from your average score by simply reducing the number of short-game shots you now play. To use this chart, first determine the total number of putts, less-than-full approach shots and sand shots from greenside bunkers you now take in an average round. Locate the column on the chart atop which your total appears. Next, determine how many short game shots you think, through your improvement, you could save out of every 20 that you now try. Locate this number on the left-hand side of the chart. The number that appears where the two columns you have chosen happen to intersect represents the number of strokes by which you would reduce your average 18-hole score.

Other players who were considered light hitters, such as Harry Cooper and Ralph Guldahl, averaged around 240. Medium-length players, such as Byron Nelson and Lawson Little, averaged 255 to 260. Craig Wood and Horton Smith were closer to 265. Ben Hogan, at that stage in his career, and others, like Chick Harbert or Jimmy Thompson, were exceptionally long, closer to 270 or even higher. Sam Snead, I feel, was the longest of them all, on average, because he was so consistent.

Still, despite my lack of length, relying heavily on my short game, I managed to win 24 tournaments on the PGA tour plus another 35 to 40 sectional competitions. I was leading money winner in 1933–34 and 1937–38. Twice, in 1934 and 1938, I won the PGA Championship itself.

At 71, I am still extremely confident about my short game. I still feel that my stroke-saving methods from within 60–70 yards of the green and on the putting surface itself will more than offset any lack of distance on long shots.

I feel the chipping technique that I first devised as a caddie in Hot Springs is especially efficient. For example, I once computed that on shots from four feet or less off the green, given a normal contour and condition of putting surface, I could hole out in an average of 1.97 strokes. I could sink my chip shot a bit more frequently than I would leave myself with two putts.

Regarding putts, during an extended period in the 1930's, my average was a fraction over 30 per round—almost six under a two-per-hole average. Later, when I adopted the unique split-hand technique that I still use on short putts—and will explain later in this book—my average dropped to a little under 29 per round.

On pitch shots from, say, 10 to 60 yards off the green, I still feel that I need some practice if, on average, I leave myself with two putts more often than one.

Perhaps you may feel that you could never become this efficient on your "part shots." Maybe you can; maybe you cannot. However, I will say this: I firmly believe that within every golfer there is a vast untapped potential for improving his short game and, therefore, his scoring.

Consider your own game. Think about a typical round at the course

Number of part shots you think you can save out of every 20 you play (Improvement %).	Average number of part shots you currently attempt every 18 holes (include all putts, all less-than-full approach shots and all shots from greenside sand bunkers).										
	40	42	44	46	48	50	52	54	56	58	60
1 of 20 (5%)	2.0	2.1	2.2	2.3	2.4	2.5	2.6	2.7	2.8	2.9	3.0
2 of 20 (10%)	4.0	4.2	4.4	4.6	4.8	5.0	5.2	5.4	5.6	5.8	6.0
3 of 20 (15%)	6.0	6.3	6.6	6.9	7.2	7.5	7.8	8.1	8.4	8.7	9.0
4 of 20 (20%)	8.0	8.4	8.8	9.2	9.6	10.0	10.4	10.8	11.2	11.6	12.0
5 of 20 (25%)	10.0	10.5	11.0	11.5	12.0	12.5	13.0	13.5	14.0	14.5	15.0

where you play most frequently. Specifically, total the number of part shots you would now be likely to take. Add together your putts, approach shots on which you make a less-than-full swing and the number of sand shots from greenside bunkers.

Once you have that total, estimate how much you think you can improve your short game. Ask yourself, "Out of every 20 part shots I now take, how many could I eliminate by improving my putting, chipping, pitching and sand play?" Eliminating one out of every 20 part shots would be a five percent improvement; two out of 20, 10 percent.

Finally, check the accompanying chart. It will tell you how many strokes you can cut from your average score, if you do, in fact, improve as much as you think you can.

I suspect that you will be surprised by the number. For instance, if your average score is now, say, 96, you may be taking some 50 part shots per round. If you could eliminate just three putts, short approach shots or sand shots from every 20 you now take, your average score would drop from 96 to 88.5!

I feel that women will find this book particularly helpful. You might think that women golfers would be exceptionally skillful on less-than-full shots, where the priority is on deftness and touch rather than size and strength. Generally speaking, this is not true, even at the professional level. At the risk of sounding chauvinistic, I have found that women golfers on the whole are vastly inferior when it comes to the short game. For instance, they seem to be less observant of such variables as whether or not the greens have been mowed that day. They seem less skilled in their ability to anticipate how terrain will affect a given shot. They seem less aware of what to expect in terms of trajectory from various clubs.

There are many exceptions, of course. Gene Littler, who has had an outstanding career in professional golf, would love to play his part shots as well as his mother, Dotty, does. She is an absolute magician around the greens. Still, I would have to say that most women desperately need to improve their short-game skills, both in their mental approach and their physical execution.

One of my aims in this book will be to help you understand short-game techniques that, quite frankly, are probably better than you now are using. They may, on occasion, seem radical, but they are all based on sound, scientific principles.

For instance, in putting I will be highly specific in the way that I think you should hold the putter and set up to the ball. Only by being specific can I provide you with a technique that reduces to the barest minimum any chance of your moving the putterhead off line or misaligning the putterface.

Once you learn to hold the putter and set up to the putt in a way that greatly reduces your chances of putting off line, you will be free to concentrate, instead, on making the ball roll the correct distance.

At times I may seem overly specific in my instruction. So be it. Contrary to some instructors, I believe that developing a consistently successful short game does not allow much leeway for personal idiosyncrasy. To apply scientifically sound principles successfully, the application must be specifically correct time after time. Where better to be specific in our technique than on short shots, where success depends so much on pinpoint directional accuracy and exactness of distance control?

Many golfers find the short game confusing. There are so many variables, so many shots of varying lengths, from so many differing lies of the ball in the grass, to so many greens that vary in texture and terrain. There are so many shots that could be played, and clubs that could be used in a given situation. There are so many ways to make a ball behave on a shot with a given club.

Golfers who disregard these variables do simplify their approach to the short game. However, they also vastly limit their potential success. The accomplished golfer understands the variables and reacts accordingly. He learns to play a variety of shots and then chooses and plays the shot that will give him the best chance for success in the situation at hand.

Indeed, I firmly believe that if you do not know how to play the part shots in golf, you really don't know how to play golf.

In this book, I will explain the variables as well as the techniques you will need to handle them. Hopefully you will, as a result, increase the number of options that you have for handling a given situation around the green.

For instance, let us assume that your ball is barely off the putting surface, say a foot or two into the fringe. The hole is some 70 feet away. In this situation, given a good lie and a well-cropped apron, at least 95 percent of the world's golfers would choose to roll the ball to the hole with a putter.

Yet there is another option, and it is the one I would choose. I would play a chip shot with a relatively straight-faced iron, such as a 4-iron or

5-iron. And, on average, I would make my shot finish closer to the hole than would the vast majority of those players who choose the putter. In fact, I would finish closer with the 4-iron than I would if I, myself, had chosen the putter.

I would be more successful for two reasons:

First, most golfers—myself included—rarely face a 70-foot putt. Therefore, the golfer who chooses to putt from just off the green at 70 feet is probably playing a relatively unfamiliar shot.

Second, I have confidence in my chipping technique. I believe that at this distance I have better directional and distance control with a chipping club than with a putter. Because I have this confidence in my chipping ability, I have an additional option that others might lack. In this book I will attempt to help you develop this same option and many others. Again, the more options you have in your repertoire, the greater your chances will be to play the one, singularly appropriate shot that is most likely to succeed at the time.

Before I close this general discussion, I would like to mention a few more reasons why you should improve your short game.

First, it is something you *can* do. Not all of us have the ability to add 20 yards to our drives, but we all can improve our putting, chipping, pitching and sand play.

Second, the work you do on your short game, especially your short pitch shots, will automatically improve your full shots. The rhythm and balance and pace of motion that you develop on part shots carries over into the longer shots. In fact, you will make more good shots with your fairway woods and long irons after a half hour's practice on 40- to 50-yard pitch shots than you would if you spent the same time actually hitting full shots with those clubs!

Third, apart from improving your full shots technically, a sound short game also improves your mental attitude toward the longer shots. Conversely, the golfer who lacks confidence in his short game puts a tremendous burden on himself when it comes to playing full shots to the green. He senses that missing the green will quite probably cost him at least one stroke. He suspects that he must put his full shot very close to the hole to avoid three-putting, and that even an exceptional approach shot will not guarantee his one-putting. All of this negative thinking increases his tension level and makes a successful full shot even more unlikely.

Fourth, a bad short shot is more disturbing than a bad full shot. What is more exasperating than three-putting from 15 feet or taking four shots to get down from just off the green? What is more exhilarating than sinking that same 15-footer to save par or make a birdie, or to run one in from off the green? And what about the emotional carry-over that leads to better full shots on the holes ahead?

Fifth, failure or success in your short game also has a direct effect on the morale of your opponents. Nothing can put you on the defensive faster than an erratic short-game performance that costs you a hole you should have won. On the other hand, a long, straight drive on your part might put a bit of pressure on your foe, but not nearly to the degree as will a chip or pitch shot that finishes next to the flagstick, or a long putt that drops into the hole.

A classic example of this occurred in the 36-hole final match of the 1938 PGA Championship at the Shawnee-on-Delaware (Pa.) Country Club. My opponent was Sam Snead who could, and did, regularly outdrive me by at least 30 to 35 yards.

The course had four par-5 holes. Sam could reach three of them in two shots and finish within 10 to 15 yards of the other. I could not possibly reach any of these greens in two shots.

However, before the match concluded, I had birdied six of the seven par-5 holes that we played. I had won all six from Sam, and parred the other par-5 without a single shot ever finishing in the fairway. Thus, I one-putted all of those longer holes.

Obviously, my short game served me well that day and, I'm sure, adversely affected Sam's play. At the presentation ceremonies, after losing 8 and 7, he was very gracious and droll. "I saw it, but I don't believe it," he said.

Finally, I would like to make one final observation, particularly to those readers who occasionally suffer from nervousness on short putts and, perhaps, on all short-game shots. Do not be ashamed of "choking."

I believe it was my friend, Dr. Cary Middlecoff, who once observed that any golfer who has never choked on the golf course should be in an asylum. In a way, he's right. Sooner or later all normal human beings encounter situations on the course that they are not, at that particular moment, emotionally capable of handling. More often than not, these attacks of nervousness occur on the part shots rather than on full shots where we are allowed to make a full muscular effort.

I feel that overcoming anxiety in golf, if not in all other aspects of life, comes first with understanding what to do—knowledge—and, thereafter, properly applying this understanding.

I think you will find that this book gives you the understanding of correct short-game technique as well as the tools to apply it correctly. If you will do your share in working toward mastering the methods that I teach, I know that your confidence around and on the greens will increase and your nervousness will begin to wane.

In the end, I hope you will look on the short game as I have throughout my golfing life. I hope you will begin to regard it not so much as a defensive tool for keeping your scores from skying, but rather as an offensive weapon for beating the course and demoralizing your opponents.

SECTION 1: PART-SHOT CONCEPTS

To become a maestro of the short game, you must first understand certain concepts. Some of these may seem a bit elementary and obvious to the experienced player. Most of them, however, will not. I have found that even veteran golfers, in most instances, lack at least some of the understanding they need to build a total short-game program, one that allows them to apply fully all of the shotmaking talents they have developed over the years.

Therefore, I hope you will carefully study the text and Tony Ravielli's illustrations that appear in this concepts section. They form a foundation that will make it much easier for you to understand and apply correctly the instruction that follows later.

Shot Elements

When you think about it, there are only three basic elements to a golf shot, as shown in *Illustration 1*.

One is its *direction*. This includes the direction in which the ball happens to start out, the direction and degree that it might happen to curve to the left or right while in flight and any sideways bouncing and rolling that might occur after it lands.

A second element is the shot's *trajectory*. This includes the upward angle of movement that the ball takes upon leaving the clubface, the amount that it climbs thereafter and the angle at which it drops to the ground.

Third is the shot's *length*. A shot's overall length is a combination of the distance that the ball carries forward through the air—its "air length"—plus the distance it bounces and rolls forward after landing—its "ground length."

All short-game shots involve at least two of these three elements—direction and length. The third element, trajectory, occurs on all normal "part shots," except putts. (Strictly speaking, even a putt may include an infinitesimal amount of carry or air length before the ball touches down on the green. However, the distance it flies is so short that trajectory can be eliminated from putting discussions.)

Take a moment to visualize each of these elements. Visualize various shots going in different directions, at different trajectories and different distances. Your eventual success at the short game will largely depend on your ability to visualize beforehand the direction, trajectory and length of the shot you plan to play.

As you visualize different shots, one thing should become apparent: There is a somewhat direct relationship between a shot's trajectory and its ground length. A high shot that drops downward to the ground at a fairly steep angle will usually not bounce and roll as far forward as will a shot that approaches the ground while flying more forward at a shallower angle.

1. Elements of a golf shot

Most golf shots include the elements of direction, trajectory and length. *Direction* is the leftward, rightward or on-target course the ball takes after it is hit, its path as it curves sideways in flight and bounces and rolls upon landing. *Trajectory* is the shot's upward-downward movement. Putts do not include this element to an appreciable extent. *Length* is the overall distance the shot travels. It is a combination of "air length" and "ground length." Success with the short game requires that you learn to visualize these elements before you play any given shot.

DIRECTION

TRAJECTORY

LENGTH

AIR LENGTH   GROUND LENGTH

Shot Influences

Thus far I've described only the three things that happen *after* the ball has been struck. Now I will explain how these elements are influenced by what happens *as* the ball is struck.

This is vital information because what the clubhead does to the ball directly determines the direction, trajectory and length of the shot. For you to understand what makes your short game shots behave as they do—and to make them do what you plan for them to do—you must first understand the various ways that the club influences what the ball does.

Apart from wind and terrain, there are five things that influence a shot's direction, trajectory and length. All involve the state of the clubhead at that split second when it is in contact with the ball. These influences are the club's (1) effective loft, (2) angle of approach, (3) path of movement, (4) face alignment and (5) speed of movement.

Effective loft. Most golfers know that a club's "loft" is the degree that its face looks upward. They know that a sand wedge has more loft than a pitching wedge—actually about six degrees more—so that a well-struck sand wedge shot flies the ball higher, but not as far, as a well-struck pitching wedge. They know that the pitching wedge has more loft—about four degrees—than a 9-iron. Thus pitching-wedge shots, again if struck solidly, fly higher but shorter than 9-iron shots. The 9-iron usually has about three degrees more loft than the 8-iron, and so on down through the set. Even a normal putter has at least a degree or two of loft.

However, these are the lofts built into the club by the manufacturer. The point you should understand is that a club's "built-in" loft can be changed—and usually is to some extent—by the actual positioning of the club when it strikes the ball (see *Illustration 2a*).

The amount of loft that the club happens to be carrying when it actually contacts the ball is its "effective loft." An 8-iron's built-in loft can actually be altered in various ways so that by contact its effective loft is equal to the built-in loft of anything from a sand wedge to a 2-iron, or even a putter (see *Illustration 2b*).

Obviously, effective loft is more important than built-in loft. It *directly* affects whether the ball flies on a relatively high or low trajectory, which, in part, determines how far a shot flies (air length) and how far it bounces and rolls (ground length).

Angle of approach. This influence on shots refers to the degree that the clubhead is moving either downward toward the ground, parallel with the ground or upward from the ground when it meets the ball.

The angle of approach is downward when contact occurs during the latter stage of the downswing. If contact takes place a bit later, just after the downswing has finished, the club's angle of approach is practically level with the ground. If it occurs still later, the club will be moving into the ball on a slightly upward angle of approach.

The club's angle of approach affects the shot's trajectory. As a general rule, on solid shots with the iron clubs, the more steeply downward the angle of approach is, the lower the shot will start. This is true because the downward approach reduces the club's effective loft (see *Illustration 3a*).

This principle is especially true on short-game shots. On these shorter shots, the clubhead's speed is usually too slow to add enough height-producing backspin to the ball to offset fully the height-lowering influence of the reduced effective loft.

If the angle of approach is level with the ground, rather than downward, the club's effective loft is greater. Given solid contact, the shot will tend to fly higher (see *Illustration 3b*).

If the angle of approach is upward, the effective loft becomes still greater. An 8-iron might be carrying the effective loft of a pitching wedge, for instance.

Here, however, I must warn against the upward angle of approach. Unless the ball is teed on a wooden peg or sets high atop tall grass, even a slightly upward angle of approach all but disallows solid contact with the underside of the ball. In fact, if you tend to top or "skull" your pitch and chip shots on a low trajectory, the problem might well be that your clubhead's angle of approach is upward (see *Illustration 3c*).

Path of movement refers to the direction that the clubhead is moving when the ball leaves its face. It can be moving toward the left of target, on target or toward the right of target (see *Illustration 4*).

Please do not confuse the clubhead's path of movement with its angle of approach. Path refers to direction of movement in relation to the target—left, right or on-target; angle refers to direction of movement in relation to the ground—downward, level or upward.

Most golfers have heard the term "target line." This refers to an imaginary line that extends from the ball to the target. You stand to the side of this imaginary target line as you play a golf shot. The side on which you stand is called "inside." The area on the opposite side of the target line is called "outside."

The clubhead's path of movement has some influence on the shot's

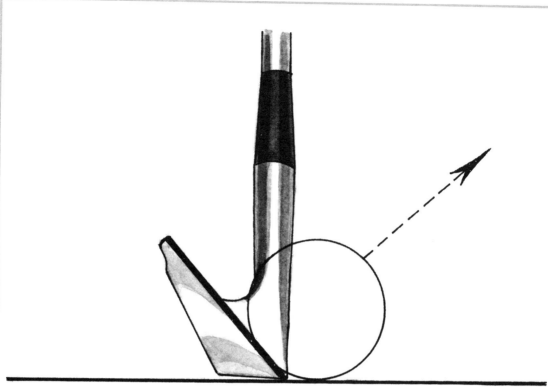

BUILT-IN LOFT

EFFECTIVE LOFT

2. Effective loft

a. *Built-in loft* is the degree that the clubface looks upward when the club is soled flat on the ground and is square to the target line. This loft is built into the club by the manufacturer and varies among the clubs in a given set.

b. *Effective loft* is the actual degree that the clubface looks upward when it contacts the ball. If the clubhead is moving downward at that time, for instance, the club's effective loft will usually be less than its original, built-in loft. Thus the shot, if struck solidly, will take off on a lower trajectory.

direction. If, for instance, it happens to be moving "on line"—straight down the target line—when it releases the ball, the shot will be more likely to fly toward the target. If it happens to be moving toward left of the target—on a path from outside to inside the target line—the shot will tend to fly to the left. The opposite path, from inside to outside the line, will tend to make it fly to the right of target, as shown in *Illustration 4.*

However, clubhead path is not the sole influence in determining the direction of a given shot. As I will explain shortly, the ball will not go in exactly the same direction that the club is *moving* if the club should happen to be *facing* in a different direction.

Clubface alignment refers to the direction that the club is facing when it releases the ball.

I prefer to relate the club's face alignment to its path of movement, rather than to the target line. Thus I would consider the clubface to be "closed" if it faces to the left of the direction it is moving. The face would be "square" if it were aligned in the same direction as the clubhead is moving. An "open" clubface is one that faces to the right of its path of movement (*see Illustration 5*).

As I just mentioned, the alignment of the clubface has some effect on the direction of the shot. If the face is aligned in the same direction as the clubhead is moving—if it is square—the ball will go in that direction unless, of course, it becomes affected by wind or terrain.

If, however, it faces to the left of its path of movement — if the face is closed—the ball will start out to the left of the direction the clubhead is moving. It will also curve even farther left because a closed clubface makes the ball sidespin in that direction. This spin can also make it bounce and roll still farther to the left.

Conversely, if the clubface alignment is open—facing to the right of its path of movement—the ball will tend to start out to the right of that path. It may also curve and bounce and roll even farther to the right because of any sidespin applied to the ball.

It is more difficult, however, to make short shots slice to the right in flight than it is to make them curve to the left.

While clubface alignment affects a shot's direction, it also has much

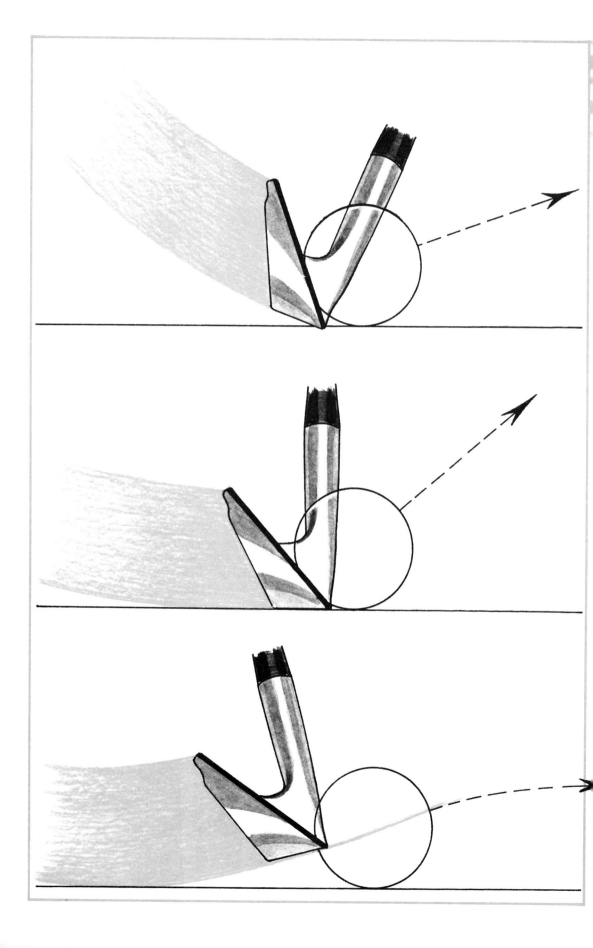

3. Angle of approach

a. *Downward angle of approach* of the clubhead at contact makes the effective loft less than the club's built-in loft. The shot starts out on a lower trajectory.

b. *Level angle of approach* with the same club makes its effective loft at contact approximate its built-in loft. The shot, if struck solidly, takes off higher than if the angle of approach is downward.

c. *Upward angle of approach* can make the club's effective loft greater than its built-in loft. However, the upward approach is suitable only on tee shots when the ball sets on a peg. It will usually produce stubbed, skulled or topped shots when the ball is not teed.

TARGET

TARGET LINE

BALL

4. Clubhead path

The club can contact the ball while moving either to the left of target (*upper path*), on target (*middle path*) or to the right of target (*bottom path*). The direction in which it is moving at contact has some effect on the direction that the ball starts out.

to do with its trajectory and length.

If you were to take a club, say a 9-iron, and sole it normally on a flat surface, you would be able to see its normal, built-in loft. However, if you were simply to turn that club clockwise so that its face alignment was opened to the right, you would see a gradual increase in its loft. Close it far to the left and you would see a dramatic decrease in its loft.

This means that shots struck with the clubface opened to the right of its path of movement fly on a relatively high trajectory. This happens, again, because the opening of face increases the club's effective loft.

Shots struck with an open clubface, because of their higher trajectory, usually have less ground length than normal. They settle and stop sooner upon landing. Shots struck with a closed face usually fly lower and, therefore, bounce and roll farther than normal—more ground length.

Clubhead speed is something that most golfers would like more of on their full shots. Given solid contact, the faster the club is moving at impact the farther the shot will go. Of course, a misdirected shot will go farther off line.

Also, the faster a club is moving the more spin it will apply to the ball. If the shot is struck with a square clubface, the added backspin will make it fly higher and stop sooner upon landing. However, if the shot is struck with an open or closed clubface, the extra clubhead speed will increase sidespin as well as backspin. The shot will fly still higher, but will also curve sideways to a greater extent (*see Illustration 6*).

In the short game, however, where shots are less than full, the goal is not *maximum* clubhead speed. Instead, the goal is the *correct amount* to make the ball finish in or near the hole. What that correct amount will be on a given shot will depend on such variables as the distance to the target, the trajectory you wish the shot to take, the club you have chosen and the amount of spin, if any, you would like to put on the ball.

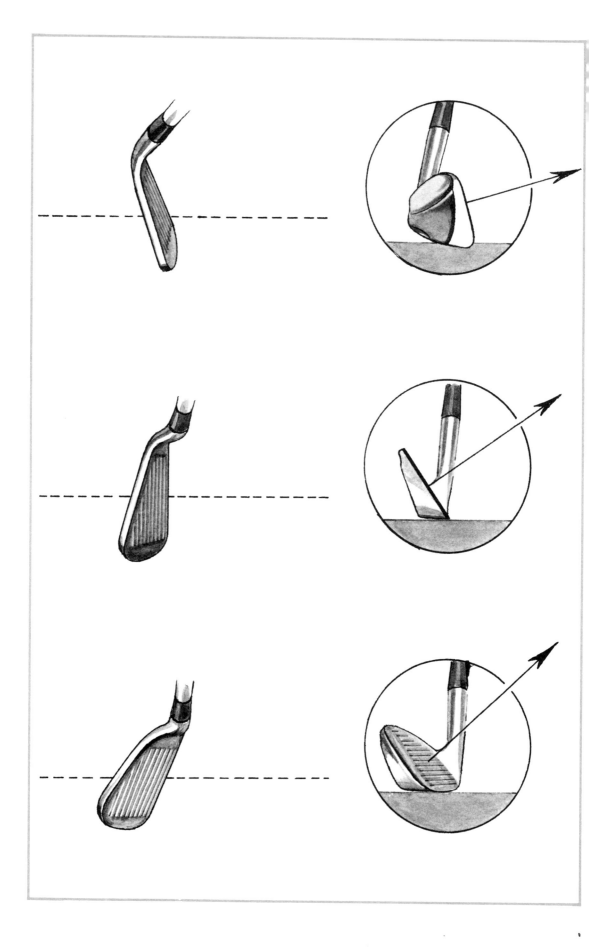

5. Clubface alignment

a. *Closed clubface.* When the clubface is closed at contact, so that it faces to the left of the direction it is moving, the shot will start out to the left of that direction. It may curve, bounce and roll still farther left. It will fly lower than normal because closing the clubface to its path of movement decreases its effective loft.

b. *Square clubface.* When the clubface is looking in the same direction that it is moving at contact, the ball will start out in that direction. It will not curve in flight unless affected by wind. All things being equal, square-faced contact will make the shot fly higher than will closed-face contact with the same club.

c. *Open clubface.* When the club faces to the right of the direction it is moving at contact, the ball will start out to the right of that path. It may curve a bit farther to the right in flight and bounce and roll still farther right. Open-faced contact increases the club's effective loft and makes solid shots fly higher than normal.

LESS SPEED

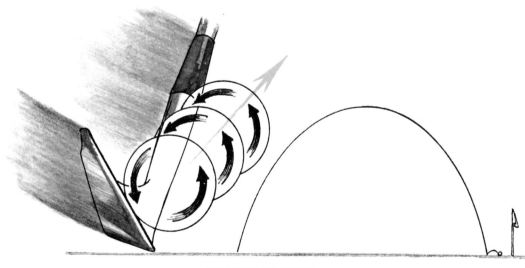

MORE SPEED

6. Clubhead speed

Clubhead speed can affect all elements of a shot—direction, trajectory and length—providing the contact is fairly solid. The faster moving clubhead will make the ball fly higher and carry farther, not only because of its additional force, but also because of the added backspin it applies. The added height and backspin may, however, reduce the shot's ground length. Added clubhead speed will also accentuate any in-flight curving to the left or right if the ball is struck with the face aligned closed or open to the clubhead's path.

Lob, Pinch,
Cut-Lob, Cut-Pinch

These terms refer to four different ways of making contact with the ball on short-game shots. It is important that you understand them because they are used throughout this book, and because once you do understand them, you will be ready to enlarge your repertoire of short-game strokes—to give yourself more options in any given part-shot situation.

Lob. A lob shot is one in which the clubhead is moving parallel with the ground when it contacts the ball. Its angle of approach is level, not downward. The club should be brushing the grass under the ball upon contacting it (*see Illustration 7a*).

Pinch. A pinch shot is one in which the clubhead is still moving downward to some degree when it contacts the ball. It meets the ball with a descending blow and then continues moving downward for a short span so that it brushes the grass or takes a bit of turf in front of where the ball was (*see Illustration 7b*).

Because the angle of approach is somewhat downward on a pinch shot, the club carries less effective loft at contact. Thus a pinch shot with a certain club will start with a lower trajectory than will a lob shot using that same club, if all other variables, such as clubhead speed and clubface alignment, are the same.

Shots can be played with varying degrees of pinch by varying the degree that the clubhead is moving downward when it reaches the ball.

For instance, it is possible to play a pitching wedge shot from off the green and make the ball fly on trajectories similar to that of an 8-iron, a 6-iron or even a 4-iron, merely by steepening the downward angle of approach and, thus, reducing the effective loft of the club.

When the pinch shot is struck solidly, it will put additional backspin on the ball. On the longer pitch shots, backspin can make the ball fly higher and stay in the air longer. However, on the shorter chip shots, where the clubhead's speed is less than maximum, the trajectory-lifting effect of extra backspin is minimal. Rarely will it be sufficient to offset the trajectory-lowering effect of decreased effective loft.

You might wonder why a person would ever want to pinch a shot. Why pinch, say, an 8-iron chip with a downward angle of approach so that it flies on the same trajectory as a 5-iron? Why not choose the 5-iron in the first place, and merely play a lob shot, with a level angle of approach so as to make the ball fly on its normal 5-iron trajectory?

The best answer to these questions is, quite simply, that the pinch shot is safer than a lob shot on most strokes played from off the green. It is safer to contact the ball with a somewhat descending angle of approach than with a level one.

You must understand that your enemy on these shots is the grass and ground behind the ball. This enemy is to be avoided as much as possible, because it can interfere with your clubhead and thus thwart it from making solid contact. The best way to avoid this enemy is to make sure your clubhead passes over it, rather than through it, as it approaches the ball. The downward angle of approach—pinching the shot—allows this clearance (*see Illustrations 7b and 7c*).

Because the pinch shot is safer than the lob shot, I prefer at least some degree of pinch on most shots from off the green. I know that even if I pinch the shot a bit too much, so that it flies even lower than I had intended, the results will usually be less disastrous than if my clubhead were to snag in the grass or the turf behind the ball.

Though I prefer the safer pinch shot on most occasions, there are times when the lob shot will give me better results. For instance, let's say my ball is just off the edge of the green. It is setting up well on the grass in a lie that will allow me to lob the shot without fear that the club's level angle of approach will cause it to snag in the grass behind the ball.

I've decided that I want to chip the ball on a 7-iron trajectory, landing just onto the green and rolling freely forward to the hole. To get this trajectory I could lob the shot with the 7-iron, or I could pinch it slightly with the 8-iron, or I could pinch it a bit more with a 9-iron, or I could pinch it severely with a pitching wedge or even a sand wedge.

In this case, because the lie of the ball is excellent, I would lob the shot with the 7-iron. Why? Because by lobbing the shot with the chipping technique I use, I would apply little or no backspin to the ball. It would be less likely to grab into the green upon landing. The more I pinched this shot, the more backspin would be applied to the ball and the more likely it would be to pull up short of the hole.

Again, however, I have the opportunity to lob this shot only because of the upright lie of the ball on the grass. Were it nestled down into the grass even slightly, as is usually the case, I could not lob the shot without running the risk of snagging my club in the grass behind the ball. Never attempt to play a pure lob shot unless the ball is sitting up extremely high on the grass. Even if the lie is average, you will be better off playing your shot with at least some degree of pinch, with the clubhead moving on at least a slightly descending angle of approach.

Too often golfers try to help their shot into the air by swinging the clubhead upward into the ball. The all-but-inevitable results are either a

a.

b.

c.

7. Lob and pinch

When the ball sets up well on the grass (a.) it is possible to play a lob shot, wherein the clubhead's angle of approach is level with the ground. If the contact is solid, the ball will take off at an angle that is similar to the club's built-in loft. When the lie of the ball is less than ideal, however (b.), it is best to pinch the shot with a downward angle of approach. Since the downward approach reduces the club's effective loft, the shot will take off on a lower trajectory. You can make a pinched shot take off on the same trajectory as a lobbed shot by merely selecting a more-lofted club initially (c.).

fat shot, where the clubhead catches in the ground behind the ball, or a low topped or skulled shot where the upward moving clubhead makes contact too high on the ball to loft it into the air on a normal trajectory.

Cut-lob and cut-pinch. Both lob and pinch shots can also be "cut" shots. You can play a cut-lob shot and a cut-pinch shot. The difference between cutting a shot and not cutting it depends on where the clubface is aligned at contact. On standard pinch and lob shots, the club is facing in the same direction as it is moving; the face is square. On cut-pinch or cut-lob shots the clubface is open, facing to the right of the direction it is moving, as it contacts the ball (see *Illustrations 8a-8e*).

For instance, you would be playing a cut shot if, at contact, your clubhead were moving to the left of target while your clubface were aligned either a bit less to the left or on target or to the right of target. If your clubhead were moving on a path that was, say, six degrees to the left of your target line while your clubface were aligned only two degrees left of that line, you would be cutting the shot by four degrees. Given the same clubhead path, if the clubface were aligned down the target line you would be cutting the shot by six degrees. If it were aligned two degrees to the right of target, you would be putting an 8-degree cut on the shot.

One big advantage in playing a cut shot is that the open clubface increases the club's effective loft. A lob shot that is also cut—a cut-lob—will fly even higher than a pure lob shot. It will settle and stop even sooner on the green.

For instance, the cut-lob with a sand wedge might be an excellent shot to play if you needed to fly the ball high over a greenside sand bunker to an extremely small landing area on the green (see *Illustration 8c*). The sand wedge would give you more height than any other club because it has more loft than any other club. Lobbing the shot would give you more height than would pinching it, because the level angle of approach creates more effective loft than does the downward angle. And cutting the shot with an open face further increases that club's effective loft.

Again, however, the lob shot, even when cut, requires an extremely

37

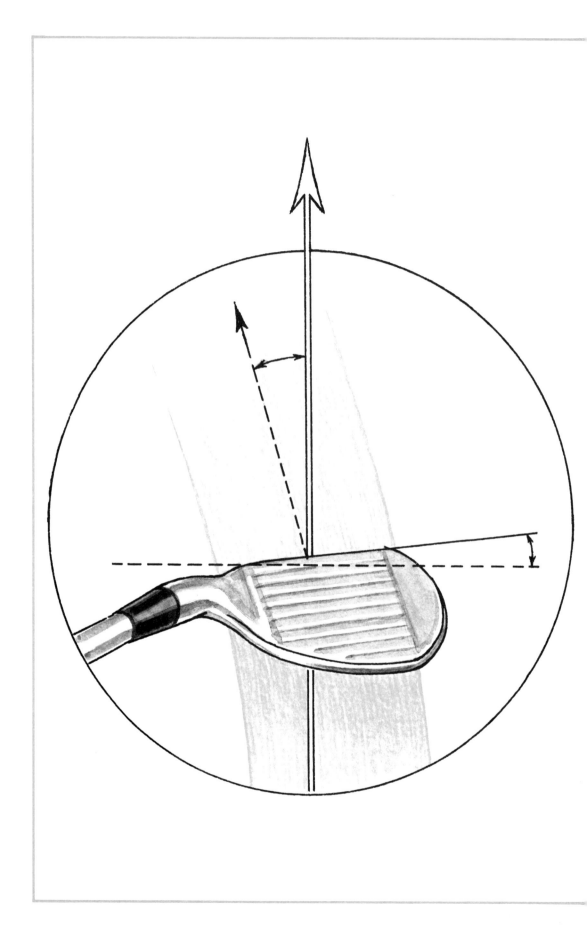

8. Cut-lob and cut-pinch shots

a. The typical cut shot finds the clubhead moving to the left of target at contact. The clubface is aligned a bit to the right of that path—it is slightly open—or, in effect, less to the left of target. The open face increases the club's effective loft and thus adds height to the shot. The shot starts out to the left of target, because the path is to the left and the facing less to the left, but then it curves and bounces to the right—back toward the hole—because of the open-faced contact. The usefulness of the cut shot is shown in the following four illustrations.

good lie with the ball setting well up on a cushion of grass.

Similarly, a pinch shot that is also cut—a cut-pinch—will fly higher and stop sooner than will that same pinch shot if it is not cut. Again, the open clubface increases the club's effective loft (*see Illustration 8e*).

The cut-pinch is an extremely valuable shot. It gives you the safety of the pinch shot, because the downward moving clubhead clears your enemy behind the ball. It can give you the height of a lob shot because the opened clubface increases the club's effective loft. In fact, you can sometimes make a cut-pinch shot actually fly higher than a pure lob shot with the same club. That would happen if the degree that you cut the shot with the opened clubface were greater than the degree you pinched it with a descending angle of approach.

There are, however, a few limitations on cut shots:

First, you can only cut a shot a certain degree. If the clubface is aligned too far to the right of its path, the shot will merely slide weakly off to the right.

Second, cutting shots with an open face does put some slice spin onto the ball. It may bounce and roll a bit to the right upon landing. On most short-game shots, however, this slice spin will seldom be sufficient to make the ball curve noticeably to the right during its flight.

Third, cutting shots with an opened clubface creates a glancing blow. A cut-lob or a cut-pinch will not fly as far as a normal lob or pinch shot wherein the clubface is squarely aligned in the same direction as it is moving. On part shots, however, this loss of length is seldom a major limitation. You could merely make a longer swing, a three-quarter swing, say, instead of a half swing.

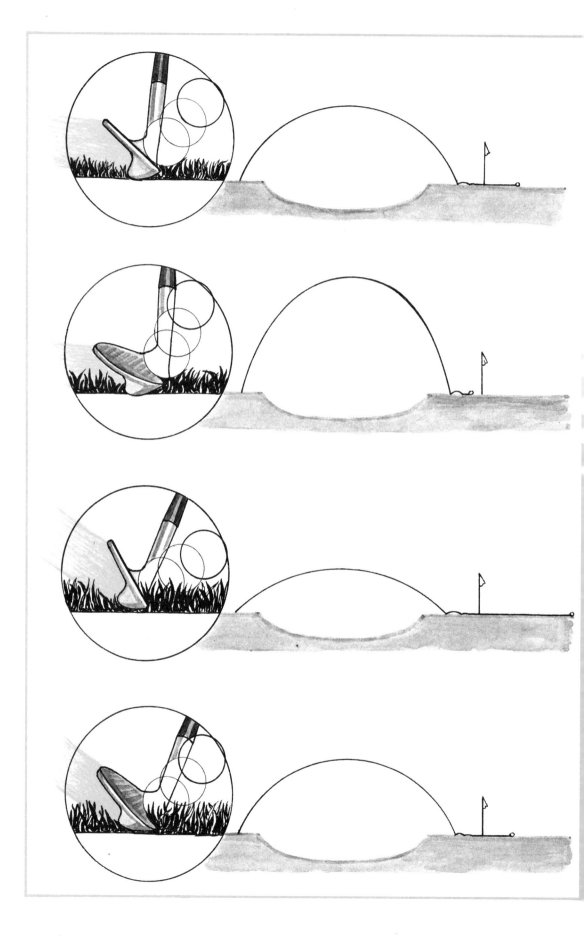

8. Cut-lob and cut-pinch shots

b. *Lob shot*. Because the ball sets atop the grass, the golfer can play a lob shot over the bunker, with a level angle of approach. Because he has lobbed the ball with his most-lofted club, the sand wedge, it flies quite high, but still runs a short distance past the hole.

c. *Cut-lob shot*. By lobbing the shot with the same club, but cutting it as well with an open clubface, the increased effective loft adds height to the shot and makes it stop sooner upon landing.

d. *Pinch shot*. Because of the poor lie, the golfer here must pinch the shot to make solid contact. The downward-moving clubhead reduces the effective loft of the sand wedge and makes the shot run far past the hole.

e. *Cut-pinch shot*. By cutting as well as pinching the shot, the golfer achieves both solid contact, despite the bad lie, and additional height, because of the opened clubface. The shot stops sooner than it does when it is pinched but not cut.

Suspension Point

The "suspension point" of your golf swing is the spot at the nape of your neck where the top of your spine protrudes slightly. Bend your neck forward and you can feel this protrusion.

I regard the suspension point as being the axis of the golf swing. The arms swing and the shoulders revolve around it. While even good players find it difficult to maintain the suspension point in a perfectly constant position as they swing on full shots, I do feel that any shifting of it should be minimal. Some shifting may be necessary to allow free swinging, but too much sideways or upward or downward movement can thwart consistently solid contact with the ball.

It should be easier for you to keep your suspension point practically steady as you play your short-game strokes because your swing will be less than full. Keeping it steady as you putt, chip and pitch not only helps insure solid contact but also gives you one other big advantage. It allows you to preset yourself *before* you swing for the type of shot you wish to play, whether that shot be a lob, a slight pinch or a severe pinch.

Once you learn where to preset your suspension point for the shot you wish to play, and once you develop the habit of holding it steady thereafter, you relieve yourself of the need to think about the mechanics of your stroke as you swing. You free your mind to focus, instead, on simply making the shot go the correct distance.

As a general rule, the farther your suspension point is set to the left at contact—the more it is ahead or leftward of the ball—the more severely you will pinch the shot. When your suspension point is to the left, the top end of the clubshaft will tend to lead the clubhead itself into the shot. This gives the clubhead a descending angle of approach into the ball, thus creating the pinch. The more the top end of the club leads the clubhead, the steeper the angle of approach becomes. As I have explained, increasing the degree of pinch by steepening the angle of approach decreases the club's effective loft. Thus, the farther to the left you set your suspension point at address, the more you will tend to pinch the shot on a progressively lower trajectory (see *Illustration 9*).

Specifically, here is how I suggest you set your suspension point to control the height of your shots:

To hit a lob shot, position yourself (1) with your suspension point even with the ball, not ahead of it or behind it and (2) distribute an equal amount of weight on each foot. Normally, this positioning will give the clubhead a level angle of approach with the ground so that solid shots fly a normal height for whatever club is being swung. Again, remember that the level angle of approach requires that the ball be in a good lie so the clubhead doesn't snag in the grass before it reaches the ball.

To pinch the shot slightly, with a slightly descending clubhead, play the ball from the same position as for the lob shot, but set your suspension point a bit farther to the left as you address the shot. Just lean to your left before you start your backswing by setting more weight onto your left foot. Leaning to the left in this manner should give your clubhead enough angle of descent into the ball to allow solid contact when the lie is somewhat less than ideal, when the ball is not setting up high atop the grass.

The worse the ball's lie happens to be, the more you will need to pinch the shot, to avoid snagging the clubhead into grass or turf behind the ball. Thus, you would set still more weight onto your left foot and thus lean your suspension point still farther to the left, as demonstrated in *Illustration 9*.

There will be many times when the lie is so tight you cannot pinch the shot severely enough by simply leaning to the left before swinging. Then you will not only need to lean to the left onto your left foot, but also to play the ball farther back in your stance. To do this, merely position yourself so your suspension point is initially ahead of the ball—to the left of it—and then lean left as well.

You can also apply the suspension point concept when you wish to play a cut shot, to make the ball fly higher and stop sooner than it normally does on a non-cut shot. The way to do this is shown in *Illustrations 10b and 10c*.

Once you have studied *Illustrations 9 and 10*, you should be able to appreciate how the suspension-point concept allows you to program yourself for the shot you wish to play *before* you swing, thus allowing you to focus solely on distance *as* you swing.

With practice, you will soon discover just how far you must set your suspension point to the left of the ball at address to achieve a given degree of pinch at contact. You will discover how much you must turn your suspension point to the left and aim the blade open to your intended swing path to achieve a given degree of cut.

This system for presetting your suspension point will work if you remember two simple things:

First, always position your hands in the same spot, opposite your left thigh, regardless of how much you lean to the left, and play the ball back in your stance to the right. This is necessary so that in varying the position of your suspension point in relation to the position of the ball you

43

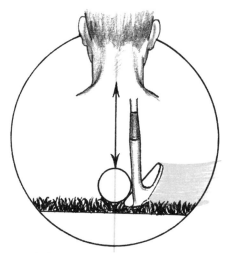

a. LOB SHOT—EXCELLENT LIE

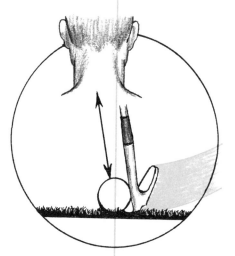

b. SLIGHT PINCH

c. ADDITIONAL PINCH

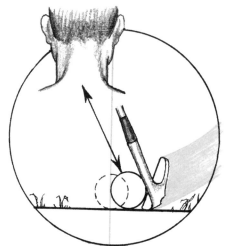

d. BAD LIE—PLAY BALL TO RIGHT IN STANCE

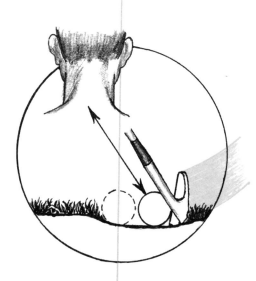

e. BAD LIE—PLAY BALL STILL FARTHER RIGHT

9. Suspension point (lob, pinch)

You can preset your suspension point—the bump at the nape of your neck—at address to produce the angle of approach you need to contact the ball solidly, rather than the ground behind it. Here we see the ball setting in five different lies of varying quality: the varying angles of approach needed for solid contact and the varying positions of the suspension point in relation to the ball that are needed to produce those angles of approach. You will note that the lob shot from an excellent lie (*a.*) is played with the suspension point even with the ball. The golfer leans to the left (*b.*) to pinch the shot slightly and still farther left (*c.*) for additional pinch. From bad lies (*d. and e.*) he must not only lean left, but also play the ball progressively farther back—to the right—in his stance.

also, in fact, vary the position of the top of the club in relation to the clubhead.

It would serve no purpose to lean your suspension point to the left to pinch a shot if you did not also move your hands, and thus the top of the club, in that direction as well.

Second, maintain a steady suspension point as you swing. Moving it to the left during the stroke would, in effect, create more pinch than you had anticipated. Moving it to the right would lessen pinch and thus increase the risk of either snagging the clubhead in the ground behind the ball or, as is often the case, catching the ball with an upward moving clubhead. If you now hit behind the ball on some chip and pitch shots and/or top or skull others along the ground or on a low, driving trajectory, you might well be either setting your suspension point too far to the right at address and/or moving it to your right during your stroke.

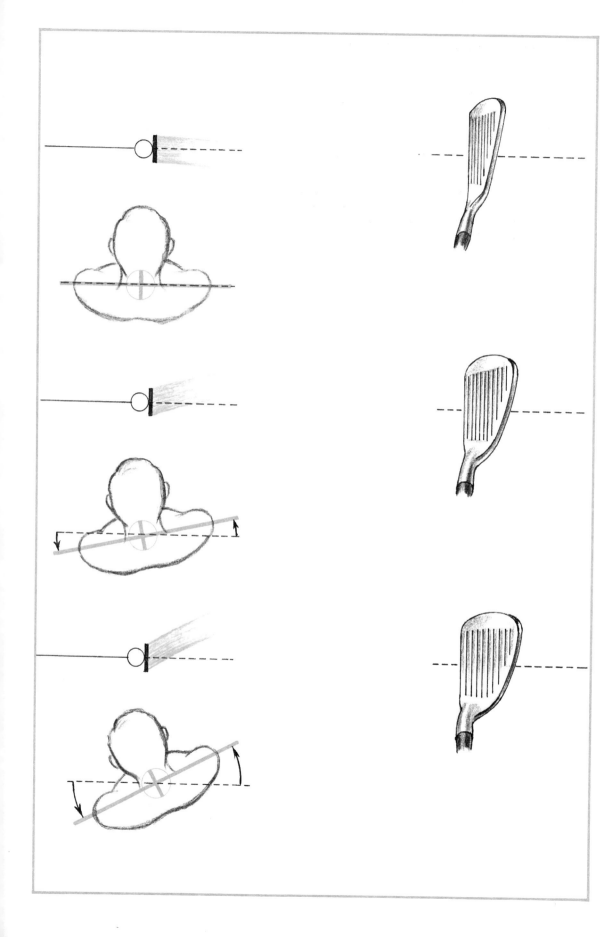

10. Suspension point (non-cut, cut shots)

a. To play a *lob or pinch shot with no cut*, align your shoulders parallel with your target line and aim the clubface down that line. This programs the clubhead to move on-target and face on-target at contact.

b. To *cut the shot slightly*, merely turn your suspension point a bit to the left at address, but aim the clubface either on-target or less to the left than you have aligned your shoulders. This positioning creates a clubhead path that is moving slightly to the left at contact but a face alignment that is open to that path. Thus the club will carry more effective loft than normal, because it is opened to the path.

c. To *cut the shot severely*, turn your suspension point more to the left at address but do not change the aiming of the clubface. This creates a clubhead path that is more leftward at contact and a clubface alignment that is still more open to that path. The still greater effective loft that results from the more open clubface produces a still higher shot trajectory.

SECTION 2: PUTTING

Compared to the rest of golf, putting looks easy. The ball always rests atop a manicured surface, inviting solid contact. There are no trees, bunkers, water hazards or out-of-bounds areas to heighten the challenge. The putting stroke itself is relatively short and elementary.

Then why does putting create so much frustration, even consternation? Why do we putt quite well one day, so horribly the next? And why do otherwise logical men and women, who dedicate so many hours each week to the sport, seldom, if ever, practice the part that uses up some 30 to 50 percent of their shots?

To some extent, I blame a common golf cliché. It holds that putting, unlike all other phases of play, allows the individual a wide latitude for doing his or her own thing. We've been told time and again that when it comes to putting, we can hold the club, set up to the ball and make our stroke in more or less whatever ways feel comfortable and seem to work.

Well, that is the worst hogwash in golf. This laissez-faire attitude has deceived us into thinking that putting is truly as simple as it looks, that there is really no right and wrong way to go about it, that technique doesn't matter all that much. It has caused us to neglect putting practice, to be haphazard about our style and inconsistent in its application—if we putt badly one day, we merely putt differently the next.

I take the opposite stand.

Putting is *not* that simple. It demands constant attention—practice.

11. Successful putting requires:

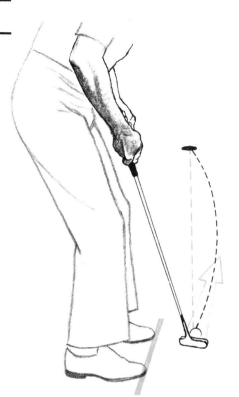

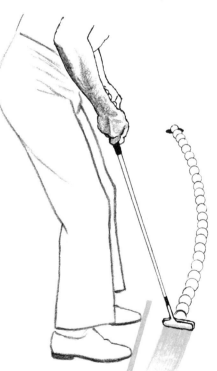

a. FINDING THE CORRECT PATH . . .

b. AIMING THE PUTTER AND YOURSELF DOWN THAT PATH . . .

c. ON-PATH CLUBHEAD MOVEMENT AT PROPER SPEED DURING CONTACT, AND . .

d. SOLID CONTACT, WHICH MEANS . . .

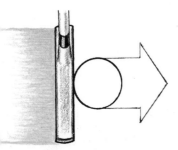

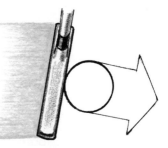

. . . PUTTERFACE SQUARE
TO PATH . . .

. . . NOT CLOSED . . .

. . . NOT OPEN . . .

. . . PUTTERHEAD MOVING
LEVEL TO GROUND . . .

. . . NOT DOWNWARD . . .

. . . NOT UPWARD . . .

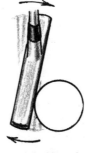

. . . CONTACT ON SWEET SPOT . . .

. . . NOT ON TOE . . .

. . . NOT ON HEEL.

Putting is a science. There are specific ways to putt that are scientifically superior to others. Precise application of a scientifically superior method will produce superior putting.

You will recall that in the section on concepts, I described the basic elements of a golf shot—direction, trajectory and distance. In putting we need not worry about trajectory; the ball does not leave the ground an appreciable amount. At least in this respect, putting is a relatively simple part of the game. It is also simplified by the fact that you need not worry about which club to select for the shot at hand.

However, direction and distance are crucial. A putt that is misdirected will surely cost you at least one stroke. So will a putt that does not travel sufficient distance, or one that is struck too forcefully.

Both of these elements are influenced on all putts to some extent by the green itself—its slope and the texture of its surface. Therefore, in this section, I will devote a chapter to reading greens and the strategy of planning putts.

Both direction and length are also influenced by the type of putter you use and the spot on its face where you contact the ball. Every putterface has a "sweet spot." If you miss that spot by as little as one-fourth to one-half an inch, a putt of, say, 20 feet or longer will roll at least two feet shorter than normal and a foot or more off line. In an upcoming chapter, I will give you some pointers about putters and how to find the sweet spot on the putter of your choice.

Finally, the same shot influences described in the concepts section—effective loft, angle of approach, clubhead path, clubface alignment and clubhead speed—all directly affect the direction and distance a putt will roll.

The goal in putting is to contact the ball with the putterhead (1) moving level with the ground, (2) moving down your chosen line, (3) facing in that same direction and (4) moving at the right speed to make the ball roll the correct distance (see *Illustration 11*).

While this is the goal, it is not humanly possible for the brain to consider all of these influences during the course of your making a putting stroke. Instead, we must find a way to more or less guarantee beforehand that these influences will be correct.

To this end, I will explain the putting grip and address position that I firmly believe is most likely to create a successful stroke *automatically*. If you will follow my grip and setup instructions to the letter, you will be more likely to contact the ball with the putterhead moving level with the ground, down your chosen line and facing square to that line.

Taking care of these influences before you stroke will leave you with only one thing to think about as you stroke. You will be free to create the right amount of clubhead speed to roll the ball the correct distance.

In short, here is a putting system that takes care of the element of direction *before* you make your stroke so that you can focus solely on the element of distance *as* you stroke.

Moreover, the grip and address positions I advocate not only free your mind to think about distance as you stroke; they also help create the type of stroke that makes distance easier to control.

Before I proceed to the chapter on putting technique, I would like to mention two more points.

First, though I stress the importance of precisely applying a putting technique that is scientifically sound, I appreciate fully that putting is an art as well as a science. I know I would be doing a disservice in the long run if I asked you to make changes that would rob you forever of the naturalness and sensitivity you have already developed.

Some things I suggest may feel foreign to you initially. So be it. In a short time, they will become natural to you, because they are, in fact, natural to the structure and function of our bodies. My suggestions are designed not only to create a scientifically sound putting stroke, but to help you make such a stroke naturally.

Second, the things I suggest you do when putting from on the green are almost identical to those I advocate when chipping from off the green. In fact, the chipping section in this book will be little more than a brief review of putting technique, with a minor adjustment for the fact that chip shots, unlike putts, do involve the additional element of trajectory.

Putting Technique

The grip and address position I advocate for putting, and for chipping as well, are designed to create a firm-wristed stroke. In these areas of the short game, wrist action serves no useful purpose. It merely decreases your chances of making solid contact with the club moving on the correct path, at the right speed. If you can learn to hold the putter and address the putt exactly as I suggest, you will have automatically reduced to the barest minimum any chance of either misconnecting with the ball and/or stroking it off your chosen line.

Flipping with the wrists makes the putterhead lift too abruptly during the backstroke, descend too abruptly during the downstroke and then flip abruptly upward again on the follow-through. All this upward-downward-upward movement reduces the duration that the putterhead is actually moving parallel with the ground at ball level. It also minimizes the duration during which the club is carrying the proper amount of effective loft. It can reduce the duration in which your clubface is aligned square to its path. It can reduce the duration during which your putterhead is moving along the line you have chosen. Most certainly, any flipping of the wrist loosens your grip, thus reducing your control of the putter.

Moreover, flipping the wrists also adds another speed-producing element to the stroke, an element that is not needed on these shorter shots. This added element makes it more difficult to control distance.

If you now putt with a wristy stroke, you may find that the change to a firm-wristed stroke will temporarily reduce your ability to control distance on your putts. However, once you become familiar with using a firmer stroking action, your distance control will become better than ever. Not only will you have eliminated an unnecessary speed-producing variable, but your contact with the ball will be more consistent. Your ability to stroke putts in the right direction will also improve, because you will have eliminated a variable that can misalign the putterface and misdirect its path of movement (see *Illustration 12*).

With wristiness eliminated, the stroke you should arrive at is one in which the whole job of moving the putter back and forward is given over to your arms. Your hands will merely hold onto the club *firmly*, each with

54

an *equal amount of pressure* that remains *constant* throughout the stroke.

It will be a stroke in which each forearm shares equally in moving the puttershaft back and forward, each pushing or pulling with an *equal amount of effort* and, most important, each *directing that effort in the same direction*.

If your arms work together equally, each directing its efforts in the same direction, and if your hands grip with equal and constant pressure, the club will move on a consistent path and the clubface will always be square to that path.

However, the path on which I think your putter should move back and forward is *not* a perfectly straight line.

I'm sure you are aware that on full shots with longer clubs, the clubhead arcs around your body to some extent. It may start back away from the ball straight along your target line, but then it gradually moves more and more to your side of that line—the inside—as it swings back and up. During the downswing it arcs back to the line before returning to the inside after contacting the ball.

It is natural that your putting stroke should follow this same pattern, but to a lesser degree. Though you do stand closer to the ball when putting than on full shots, you still must stand to the side of it. For this reason, it is natural that your putterhead move a bit to the inside during your backstroke, then back to the line as it returns to the ball. The extent that it moves to the inside will depend on the length of your stroke. On short putts, where the stroke is relatively short, the putterhead may not leave your putting line a noticeable amount. On long putts, however, it might move an inch or more to the inside before your backstroke is completed.

On these longer putts, especially, attempting to move the putter back on a perfectly straight line requires an unnatural maneuvering of the arms and hands. This maneuvering must then be reversed perfectly—and, again, unnaturally—during the forward stroke to return the putter back to the ball on a similarly straight path.

It is also unnatural for you to try to keep your putter facing in the same direction throughout your stroke. This requires an abnormal counterclockwise turning of your arms and hands during the backstroke and a perfect reversal during your forward swing.

Instead, it is natural and logical that the putter face square to its *path*, not to the target line, throughout the stroke. As the path moves gradually to the inside during the backstroke, the putter should gradually face more and more to the right of the putting line. Then it should gradually return to its original facing as the putterhead itself returns from inside to along the putting line during the forward stroke.

With these general thoughts in mind, refer to *Illustration 13* as I elaborate on the specifics of putting technique. These drawings show

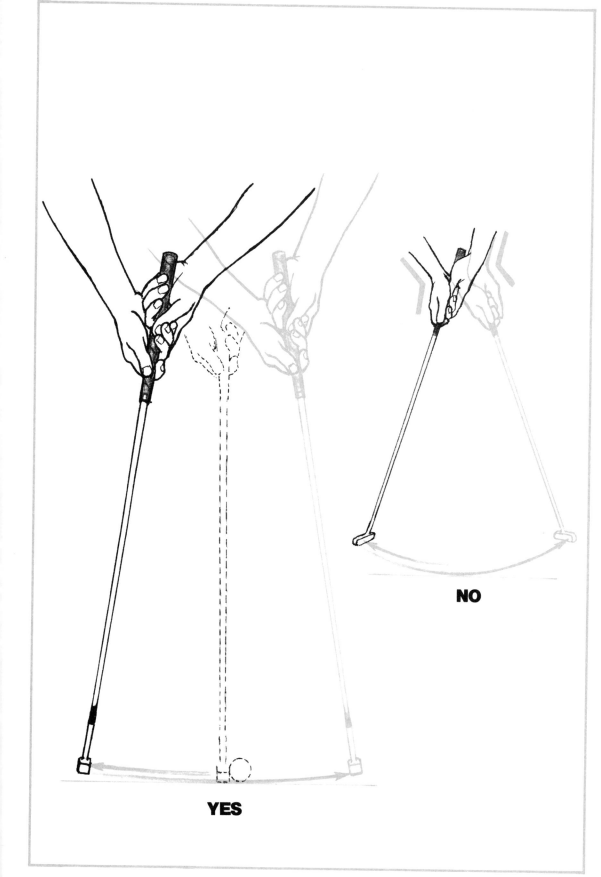

YES

NO

12. Putt with your arms . . . not with your wrists

The ideal putting stroke disallows any hinging of the wrists, but allows each forearm to do its equal share in moving the putter back and forward on the proper path. This firm-wristed stroke helps eliminate any undue change in grip pressure, any unnecessary speed-producing element and any flipping of the putterhead— either upward-downward or opened and closed—all of which are likely to occur whenever the wrists come into play.

me addressing a putt from two different angles. They are your models. Along with the more detailed illustrations that follow, they show all of the things that I feel are scientifically sound and muscularly natural about holding the putter and setting up to a putt.

Again, I believe that if you can adopt the positions I assume before putting, to the point that they feel natural to you, you will have accomplished all that is humanly possible to strike putts solidly in the right direction. You then will have created a situation that frees you to focus solely on the one remaining element—distance—as you actually make your stroke.

Arms. In the firm-wristed stroke, the arms must do the job of moving the putter. Thus, their positioning at address is critical, both in relation to each other and in relation to the club itself.

If you are right-handed, your left forearm should be set directly in front of the puttershaft. Your right forearm should be directly behind it (see *Illustration 14a*). If you were to add an extension to the top of the shaft so that it continued upward between your arms to your stomach, both forearms would parallel that extension. Neither would be above or below it. Put another way, if a spike were driven horizontally through your forearms, it would pass directly through this shaft extension.

When your forearms oppose each other in this way, directly in front of and behind the shaft, they are in perfect position for each to do its fair share in channelling power directly through the shaft to move it on a proper path with the putterface remaining square to that path.

This would not be likely to happen naturally if the shaft extended either above or below both of your forearms. Then, if you moved your arms on a correct path, they could not be channeling force directly through the shaft.

Nor would it happen naturally if you set one arm higher than the other at address. For instance, if you set your right arm higher than your left, as so many golfers do, that imaginary spike through your forearms would extend downward and off to the left, away from your target line. As you stroked through the ball, you might stroke in that direction, off to the left. Or you might correct yourself during your stroke, lowering the right

13. Model address position for putting

The ideal address position for putting is shown here in full-figure illustrations. Various particulars of the address position are shown in the more-detailed illustrations that follow in this section. By adopting all aspects of pre-stroke positioning, you can preset yourself to putt the ball in the right direction automatically, without conscious mental effort. This frees your mind to focus solely on distance as you actually swing the putter.

14. Position of arms

a. The goal is to set the forearms so each can direct an equal force directly through the puttershaft, pushing and pulling it back and forward on the correct path. They should be positioned directly in front of and behind the shaft so the shaft, if extended upward, would run directly between them (large illustration). You cannot direct equal force through the shaft in the right direction if this extension would run above or beneath the forearms, or if either arm is set above or below the extension (smaller illustrations).

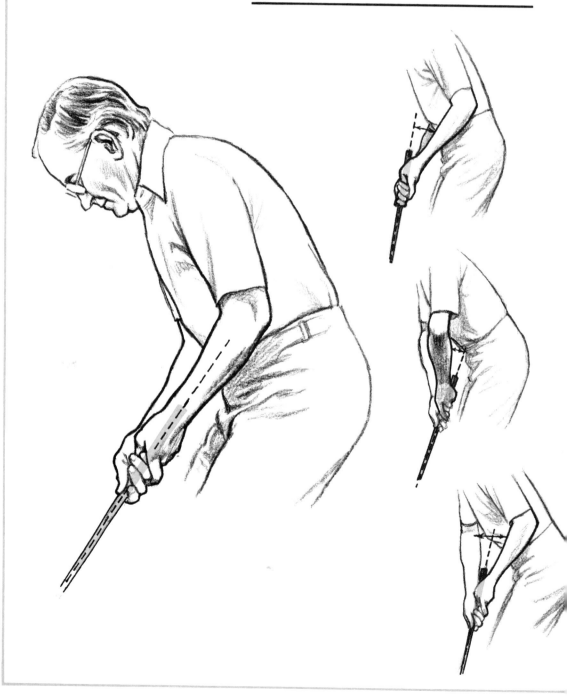

b. Not only should the forearms be directly in front of and behind the imaginary shaft extension, but each should angle down to the shaft at 45 degrees (large illustration). If this angling is less than 45 degrees, you will need to stand too tall—too far from your work—(upper-smaller illustration), or to grip too far down on the shaft. If the angle formed between each arm and the shaft is more than 45 degrees (lowest illustration), your elbows will be forced outward so they inhibit free arm movement—you will be forced to rely on your hands and wrists instead—and you may be forced to grip the putter too tightly to retain control of it.

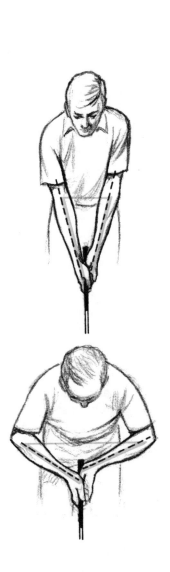

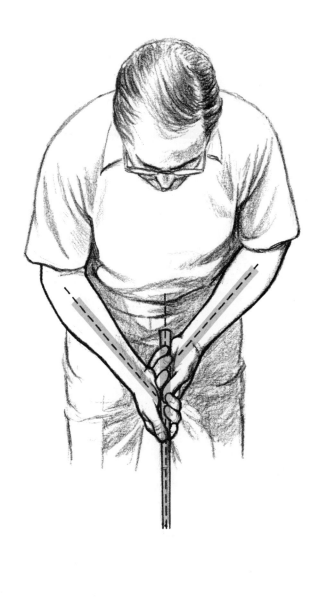

arm and raising the left so that they were, in fact, level upon contacting the ball. However, in making this correction, you would naturally be forced to turn your putterface to the right, so that it aligned in that direction at contact.

The opposite occurs if you address the putt with your left arm higher than your right; the imaginary spike would extend out to the right, across your putting line. You might move the putter through the ball in that direction, out to the right, or you might adjust to a level arm relationship during your stroke. In that case, the putter, upon contact, would have to be facing to the left of where you had aimed it at address.

So, the first thing to remember about your forearms is that they oppose each other, directly in front of and behind the putter, with neither set higher or lower than an imaginary extension of the shaft.

There is one other aspect of arm positioning you should notice and, hopefully, adopt. Observe the angle at which my forearms join the club. An angle of about 90 degrees is formed between the arms. The shaft, if extended upward, would split this 90-degree angle. Thus each forearm approaches the shaft at an angle of about 45 degrees (see *Illustration 14b*).

This angling of the arms to the shaft is important because it determines, in large part, your overall posture at address. If the angle between the shaft and the forearms is less than 45 degrees, because the arms are too close together, you will be forced to stand too upright. This puts you too far above your work, too far from your job of making solid contact. It makes your stroke too willowy, too lacking in crispness and control of the putterhead.

You could address putts with your arms angled to the club at less than 45 degrees, however, and still assume a proper posture. But to do so, you would need to grip too far down on your putter, perhaps below the leather. This would shorten the putter to the extent that, on long putts especially, you would need to make an inordinately long or forceful stroke to get the ball to reach the hole.

The opposite extreme, angling the arms to the shaft at more than 45 degrees, forces you into an extremely crouched address posture. This is a lesser evil than standing too tall—at least it gets you closer to your work. Unfortunately, this wide angling of the arms to the shaft also weakens your hold on the club. It tears your hands away from the shaft and can lead to a willowy, uncontrolled stroke unless you greatly intensify your grip pressure. This, in turn, tightens your arm muscles and inhibits their ability to move freely back and forward, especially on longer putts that require a relatively long stroke.

Increasing the arm angles to the shaft beyond 45 degrees also tends to force your upper arms away from your side, where I think they should rest gently as you address the putt.

I have given you quite a bit of information about the wheres and whys of arm positioning in this section. However, the main points to remember are that the forearms set directly behind and in front of the club with neither being above or below the imaginary shaft extension, and that each approaches the shaft at a 45-degree angle.

Not coincidentally, the proper positioning of the two forearms in relation to the club is the same that a carpenter might use to solidly support an upright timber with two braces. Like your forearms, he would set each brace at a 45-degree angle to the timber with each directly opposed to the other. In both cases, a sturdy structure is assured.

Hands. Every golfer should have two types of grips—one that allows the wrists to hinge and unhinge freely, for all those shots that require a relatively long swing to make the ball fly relatively high and/or far. (I will describe such a grip when we get to the section on pitch shots, which do call for at least a fair amount of swing length.) The second type is for putting and chipping, shorter shots which do not require a long swing. They allow us to use a grip that encourages a firm-wristed stroke, which is best for precise contact and control of both direction and distance. In fact, if the firm-wristed stroke did not limit swing length and clubhead speed, and thus height and distance, I would use my putting-chipping grip on all shots.

The putting grip I advocate does more than merely encourage a firm-wristed stroke, however. It also *allows* you to position your arms correctly, as I have just described. You will find it unnatural, perhaps impossible, to position your arms correctly if you do not position your hands correctly. The reverse applies as well.

The ideal position for the hands when putting and chipping is for each palm to be facing inward and upward at a 45-degree angle. In other words, each palm should face midway between directly upward and directly inward toward the other (*see Illustration 15a*).

The best way for you to see and feel the logic behind this putting-chipping grip is actually to set your hands on a putter. Hold the club about three-fourths of an inch from the end of the shaft. Sole its head flat on the ground, just far enough away from your feet so that it is directly below the bridge of your nose when you bend comfortably from the knees and hips.

You should find that this grip naturally makes your upper arms want to rest lightly against your rib cage, as they should. Your forearms will set directly in front of and behind the club. The shaft will be angled toward you so an extension of the grip runs straight up to your stomach, parallel with your forearms. Neither forearm will be above or below this extension. Each forearm will angle in toward the club at an angle of approximately 45 degrees.

Please review what I have just said, study the illustrations, and adjust as necessary to see that all aspects of your grip, club and arm positions are as I've just described. If your positions are correct, you will

15. Position of hands

a. Each hand should be positioned so that the palm, if opened, would face upward and inward at 45 degrees. Thus each should face midway between directly upward and directly inward to each other. This positioning is vital so each forearm can angle down to the shaft at 45 degrees as shown in Illustration 14b. When so positioned, each hand thwarts the other from unduly opening or closing the putterface during the stroke. The grip pressure should be equally firm in each hand and should remain constant throughout the stroke.

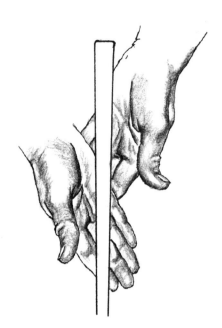

CORRECT HAND POSITIONS

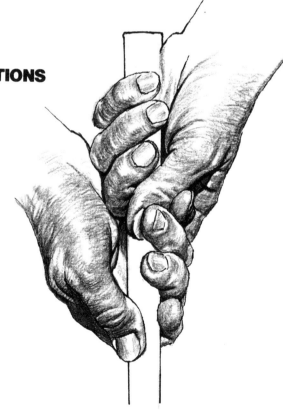

b. Here we see the problems that result when both hands are not positioned neutrally at address. If, for instance, the right hand is set correctly—facing inward and upward at 45 degrees—but the left is faced directly inward (left-hand illustrations), the putterface will be turned to the left at contact as the hands return to a neutral position. Below at right we see the opposite effect, with the left hand correctly positioned at address, but the right hand faced directly inward. In this instance, the hands again return to a neutral position at contact which forces the putter to be faced to the right. The only way to offset the natural tendency of the hands to return to a neutral position at contact is to hold the club unnaturally with more grip pressure in one hand than in the other, or to otherwise inhibit the naturalness of the stroke.

LEFT HAND PLACED INCORRECTLY

RIGHT HAND PLACED INCORRECTLY

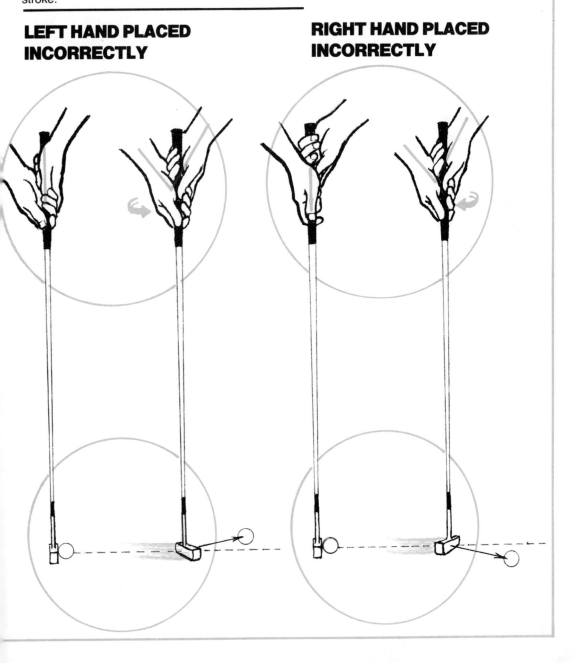

be in the most natural position possible for applying a push-pull force directly through the shaft with your arms.

Now, to appreciate why this is the ideal grip for putting, I would like you purposely to alter the position of your hands and note what happens.

First, turn your hands away from each other so they both face directly upward. As you do this, you will notice that your elbows want to press in too firmly against your rib cage. This would stifle free movement of your arms during the stroke. You will also notice that the club wants to come loose in your left hand, which would force you to grip too tightly and further impede free arm movement. You will notice, too, that the clubshaft wants to move outward away from you, so that the club begins to rest on its toe end. This sets the shaft above, not between, your forearms. The push-pull force of the arms during your stroke would no longer pass directly through it, as it should. It would be difficult to move the putter on a proper path. Hopefully this experiment will help you appreciate that facing the hands directly upward is less than ideal.

Next, I would like you to turn both hands inward. Turn them beyond the original 45 degrees until both palms actually face each other. Neither palm is now facing upward or downward.

As you make this adjustment, you should find that the shaft gradually lowers to the extent that its imaginary extension would run below your forearms. This again would make it difficult to push-pull the club with your arms in the right direction. You should find that your upper arms want to move away from your rib cage. You may feel some tension in the muscles at the back of your upper arms, tension which would inhibit your arm movement during your stroke.

You will notice, too, that your elbows have spread farther apart, thus widening the angle between each forearm and the club well beyond the prescribed 45 degrees.

Finally, you will again notice that your hands tend to loosen their hold on the club.

Thus, you can see some of the ways in which the palms-facing grip thwarts your efforts to position your arms and club in what I consider to be the ideal relationship.

There is a way for you to grip the club with your palms facing without sacrificing this relationship. You will experience that solution by merely "standing taller," by bending less from the knees and hips. Try it.

Quite honestly, there are some excellent putters who do use the palms-facing grip. I feel it is less than ideal, however, for the reasons you have just experienced. To use this grip fairly effectively, you must stand too tall at address. I feel, again, that for most people this sets them too far above their work. It reduces their ability to control the business of solidly contacting the ball with a crisp, firm-wristed stroke.

Thus far, in each of the three grips I have asked you to try, you have set your hands on the club in what I consider to be a "neutral" position. That is, each palm was faced upward and/or inward an equal number of degrees. This neutrality of hand positioning is extremely important in putting and chipping because it helps you return the putter to the same facing at contact that it was in when you aimed it at address.

Facing the palms in a neutral position creates an equal amount of resistance in each hand and arm. Each thwarts the other from opening or closing the putterface prior to contact. Thus the neutral grip allows you to push and pull equally with each arm while maintaining an equal and constant amount of grip pressure in each hand throughout the stroke. To me this is natural and ideal.

The problem with a grip in which the palms are *not* neutrally positioned at address is that they will tend to find a position at contact in which they *are* neutrally positioned. It is the change from non-neutral to neutral that misaligns the putterface and misdirects the putt.

For instance, let's assume that you set up to the putt with your right palm properly positioned, facing 45 degrees upward and inward. Fine. However, let's also assume that you did not neutralize this right-hand position by similarly setting your left palm 45 degrees upward and inward. Let's assume, instead, that you faced that palm directly inward (*see Illustration 15b*).

From this non-neutral position, your tendency during your stroke would be to split the difference. If you made a perfectly natural stroke, with each arm pushing and pulling equally, with no alteration of grip pressure, you would arrive at contact with both palms facing upward an equal amount, or 22½ degrees.

Unfortunately, during the course of returning to this neutral position, you would have necessarily closed the putterface that same 22½ degrees. The putt would roll that far left of where you had originally aimed.

Remember, our goal is to stroke each putt solidly in the right direction. This implies that the putter must be facing in the same direction it is moving; otherwise, the blow will be glancing. It also implies that the putter must be moving in the direction you have chosen for the ball to start rolling.

I feel that the arm positioning suggested in the previous section, and the hand position suggested herein will best work together in helping you achieve this goal. Moreover, they will help you do it in the most dependable way, with a firm-wristed stroke in which the arms push and pull equally in the right direction on the club itself.

Finally, I would like to stress that you hold the club with an *equal* amount of firmness in each hand—just enough to inhibit any wrist action—and that you maintain this same degree of firmness in each hand *throughout* your stroke.

16. Position of eyes

a. Setting the eyes *directly over* the putting line helps you aim the putter correctly because you are better able to see the correct line. Aiming on line helps you align your feet and body parallel to the line. This helps you stroke on the proper path, from inside to along the line.

b. When your eyes are set *inside* the ball's position, you must look out to the right to see the hole. This makes you aim the club and align yourself to the right. Your putter is then faced to the right and moving to the right at contact, at least until you tire of seeing putts finish to the right and create some compensation in your stroke to bring it back to the left.

c. When your eyes are set *outside*, beyond the line, you must look back to the left to see the hole. This line of vision makes you aim the putter and align yourself too far to the left. Initially your putter will be facing and moving to the left at contact. Soon, however, you will tire of seeing your putts finish left of the hole. Unless you correct the original error—eyes beyond the line—you will make some other compensation in your stroke to avoid missing to the left.

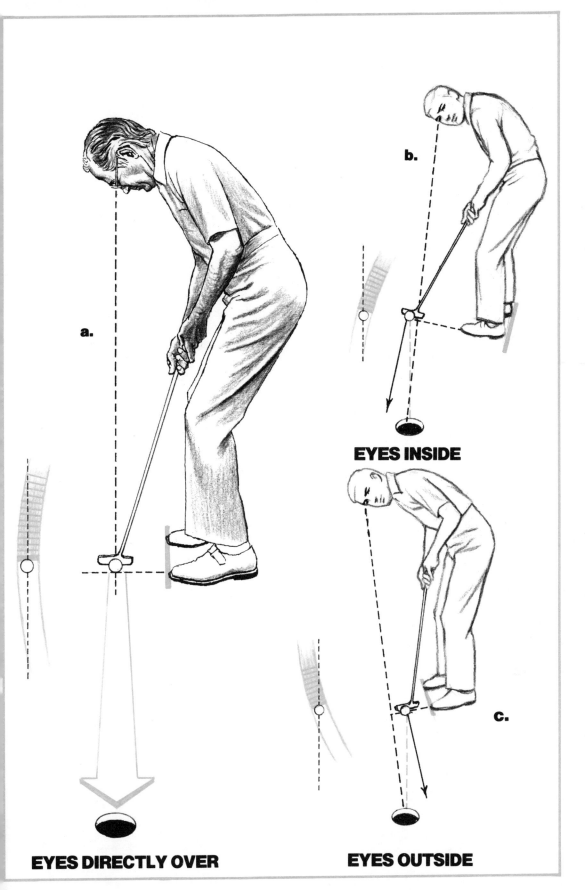

a.

b.

EYES INSIDE

c.

EYES DIRECTLY OVER

EYES OUTSIDE

Eyes. If you will pardon a quip, in putting the eyes should not be overlooked. Where you position your eyes at address can affect the direction in which you aim the putter before you stroke and where you direct it as you stroke.

You should position your eyes at address so that a line extended across them would be directly over your putting line. Setting your eyes over the line helps you see the correct line to the hole. Thus you improve your chances of aiming the putter in the right direction. Also, since we tend to adjust our stance and body alignment according to where the club is aimed, aiming correctly leads to proper stance and alignment. This, in turn, greatly simplifies your instinctive ability to stroke on line. In short, proper eye positioning helps tremendously in making the ball roll where you want it to roll (*see Illustration 16a*).

Setting your eyes out beyond the ball, over an area outside the line, tends to make you see an incorrect putting line, one that appears to be to the hole but is actually to the left. Thus, you tend to aim and stroke to the left, at least on your first attempts. Thereafter, having seen the ball finish to the left, you will still aim in that direction—because of the mispositioning of the eyes—but you may compensate by pushing your stroke out to the right of where you had aimed, thus creating a glancing blow (*see Illustration 16c*).

The reverse tends to happen when your eyes are set over an area that is on your side of the line, the inside. You will tend to misaim to the right and stroke in that direction initially. Then, seeing putts finish to the right, you will adjust by pulling your stroke to the left of where you had misaimed. The result, again, is a glancing blow. The rightward-aimed putter is swung to the left (*see Illustration 16b*).

Where you position your eyes not only affects where you aim the putter and direct your stroke, it also affects the overall shape of your stroke.

You will recall my mentioning that, because we stand to the side of the ball, the putterhead moves slightly to the inside of the line during the backstroke, noticeably so on longer putts. Thereafter, it gradually returns to the line and moves along it during contact with the ball before returning once again to the inside. You will be more likely to stroke along such a path if your eyes are set directly over the line.

When your eyes are incorrectly positioned well inside the line, you are too far away from the ball and your line. This will make the shape of your stroke too much of an arc. The putter will move too far inside the line on your backstroke and too quickly inside on your follow-through. This extreme arcing of the putterhead off the line reduces the duration that it is actually moving on the line. It dangerously lessens your chances of contacting the ball when the putter is truly moving and facing down the line.

Setting the eyes outside the line tends to change the shape of your stroke altogether. In this case, you are too close to the ball and line. Your putter may even set on its toe at address. Standing so close tends to make your putter move *outside* the line going back. Putting with this shape of stroke all but eliminates any chance of consistently stroking the ball solidly in the right direction.

Periodically check to see that you are setting your eyes directly over the putting line you have chosen. Aside from looking in a full-length mirror at home, you can do this during your practice sessions as follows: Once you have assumed your address position, while keeping your posture intact, lift your putter at the grip end with a thumb and forefinger. Let it dangle from the bridge at your nose. Hold it so that the putterhead extends lengthwise in the direction you are putting. If your eyes are properly positioned, the putterhead will cover the part of the putting line that extends immediately behind the ball.

Feet and ball positions. Where you set your feet in relation to the ball helps determine whether you will contact your putts solidly with the putterhead moving in the right direction. Also, proper foot positioning helps you aim the putter correctly in the first place.

Since you want your putter to be moving down the line when it contacts the ball, it makes sense to set your feet parallel to that line from the start. Set them so that an imaginary line across your toes would run parallel with the line on which you wish your putt to start.

Since you want to aim the putter down that line, I think it is optically advantageous to point each of your feet straight out, so that they are perfectly square to your line. You should play the ball directly opposite your left big toe—not the toe of your shoe, rather the actual big toe *in* your shoe. If you play the ball opposite that part of your left shoe, and if your left foot is pointing straight out at 90 degrees to your line, the face of your putter, if extended toward you, would run directly along the inner side of that shoe (*see Illustration 17*).

I know all this sounds rather precise, but we need to put our feet somewhere, so why not do so in a way that helps us aim the putter and ourselves correctly?

Playing the ball opposite your left toe is ideal, because there it is best positioned for contact with the putterhead as it moves level with the ground, after it has finished moving downward, just before it starts its upward movement. The level angle of approach is more likely to create solid contact and a true roll of the ball than would a downward approach, if the ball were played too far back to your right, or an upward approach, if it were played farther forward to your left.

I think that normally it is best to stand with the outer edges of your shoes closer together than your shoulders are wide, stand a bit wider—feet about shoulder-width apart—when putting in a strong wind. (If you do widen your stance in the wind, also grip a bit farther down on the club, so as to retain the 45-degree angling of the arms to the shaft.)

17. Feet and ball position

Since your goal is to have the putter moving on line at contact, it is best to set your feet equidistant from your line, so that a line across the toes would run parallel with the line itself. Setting each foot at a 90-degree angle to the line—square to it—aids in aiming the putterface similarly square. In fact, by playing the ball opposite your left big toe, you can align the putterface so it is not only square to the line, but also a natural extension from the inner side of your left foot. This ball positioning also helps insure that your putterhead will be moving level, rather than upward or downward at contact.

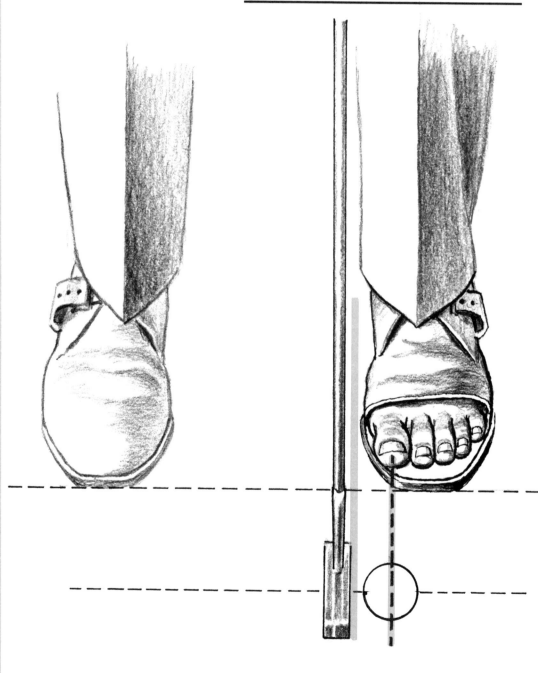

These stance widths should give you both sufficient balance and a steady suspension point as you move your arms back and forward. A stance that is too wide can lead to back and forward movement of the suspension point—swaying—which can adversely alter the path and facing of the putter. A stance that is too narrow may hinder your balance and/or make you stand too tall, too far away from your work.

Distribute your weight evenly between your two feet. Too much weight on the left foot may tilt the top of your puttershaft to the left, which will make you tend to stroke the ball with a downward moving and downward facing putterhead. Too much weight on the right foot can cause you to contact the ball when the putterhead has already started moving upward, a major cause of topping.

I find that many golfers tend to stand too far away, or they stand the proper distance away, but too tall. In either case, they are too far from their work. You will automatically stand the correct distance from the ball if you bend at the knees and well forward from the hips, and if you apply the other positions described in this chapter.

In summary, the positions you should assume when putting, so you can consider them as a whole address position, are:

Hands. Hold the club about three-fourths inch from its top end—a bit lower in a strong wind—with each palm facing inward and upward at a 45-degree angle. Hold the club firmly with identical pressure in each hand.

Arms. Upper arms rest lightly against rib cage. Forearms set directly in front of and behind an imaginary extension of the clubshaft. Neither forearm should set above or below this shaft extension. Each forearm angles downward to the shaft at a 45-degree angle.

Eyes. Directly over an extension of the putting line directly behind the ball.

Feet. Set parallel with your initial putting line, each toe straight forward at 90 degrees to that line. Outer edges of shoes slightly closer together than width of shoulders, but shoulder width in strong wind. Weight evenly distributed between feet, so that puttershaft tilts neither forward nor backward at address or at contact.

Ball. Positioned opposite where your left big toe is in your shoe.

Procedure. I have spelled out the various positions of address that I feel are ideal. You will need to fit yourself into these positions several times, each time checking to see that all are in order. After you have done this, you will begin to feel the overall sensation of what I consider to be the ideal pre-stroke positioning on putts and chip shots. In a short time, you will be able to assume these positions almost automatically, with little or no conscious effort.

I must point out, however, that while it is most important to arrive at these static positions on every putt, it is equally important that you follow a certain simple procedure in doing so. If you go about finding this ideal address position in helter-skelter fashion, it is unlikely you will find it at all.

Here then is the orderly procedure I recommend you follow in addressing every putt:

1. Set your hands correctly on the club.

2. Approach the ball from an angle that is 90 degrees to your chosen line, that is, step up to the ball with your feet pointing in the same direction they will be pointing at address.

3. Bend forward from the hips so that your eyes are over the line and set the putter lightly on the grass behind the ball, taking great care to aim it down your line.

4. Position your feet according to your line and the aim of your putter.

5. Recheck the aim of your putter and finalize your address position, making any adjustments needed to reach the ideal positioning of hands, arms, eyes and feet.

It is imperative that you learn to follow the above procedure before every putt. Most important, be sure that you aim the putter down your line *before* you position your feet. The ball and the putter, once aimed, must determine where you set your feet. If you set your feet before aiming the club, as so many do, you will aim according to where your feet are set—for right or for wrong—rather than down your chosen line.

Stroke. The whole reason for being so precise in positioning yourself correctly before stroking is simply so that you can *automatically* create a good stroke that solidly sends the ball forward in the right direction. The goal is to eliminate any need to think about *how* to stroke *as* you stroke.

If you adopt what I have suggested up to this point, you will be quite likely to make a firm-wristed stroke with each arm pushing and pulling equally on the shaft of the putter. Thus, your stroking motion and its rhythm should result from simply swinging the arms from the shoulder joints with the hands remaining constantly firm throughout. It should be a crisp, concise motion of the arms with no slackness or aggressiveness occurring in the hands and wrists.

While I feel it is inadvisable to think about your stroke as you stroke, I do believe that something must occupy your mind. Hopefully, it will be a positive image, such as that of the ball rolling into the hole, rather than the ball missing to the side, running far past or coming up far short. Our bodies tend to produce physically more or less what the mind imagines, right or wrong. In the following chapter, I will talk more about the mental focus I feel is best on different types of putts.

Putting Tactics

If there has been one thing common to all great putters over the years, it has been their determination to stick with one method and one overall game plan through thick and thin.

Even the best have their bad days on the greens. Seldom, however, do they let such occasional suffering lure them into changing their style or their strategy. They seem to realize that success is a matter of putting well *on average*—not on a daily basis or even a weekly or monthly basis, rather on a career basis. And they seem to sense that a consistent approach is the only way to achieve that goal.

I believe that Horton Smith was the best putter the world has ever seen. His physical technique was far better than adequate, but not, in my opinion, ideal. His palms-facing grip, for instance, forced him to stand a bit too tall over the ball, a bit too far from his work.

But Horton was adamant in the belief that he had a fine style. Equally as important, he refused to depart from his strategic approach, which was to visualize all putts as being straight-in. (On a breaking putt he would first decide on the direction the ball must start out to eventually curve to the hole. Then he would "move" the hole sideways in his mind's eye to a point that was straight on line with that initial putting direction.)

It made no matter to Horton if he missed, say, five or six straight putts to the left of the cup. He would never vacillate. Rather than adjust, he would simply keep on putting the ball with the same positive stroke the way he thought it should be stroked. Before you knew it, he had holed five or six in a row.

The importance of sticking to your guns on the greens was brought home dramatically to me during the 1934 Florida Year-Round Open at the Miami Biltmore course in Coral Gables. Before the tournament that year, Gene Sarazen convinced the officials they should enlarge the holes to eight inches in diameter. He said that the larger cups would take the onus off putting and give the great shotmakers an advantage he felt they deserved.

I disagreed. I maintained that while the less-skilled putters would make more putts, so would the good putters. The relationship would remain the same.

Also, I decided beforehand that I would not change my own putting strategy one iota. I would continue to lag my longer putts, just as I always had, despite the larger targets.

In the end, my refusal to change paid off. I won the tournament by 11 shots, shooting 263, which was 25 under par. I did not three-putt a single green in 72 holes. Charlie Guest was the only player who three-putted just one green. He finished second.

The others fell prey to the siren's call. Tempted by the larger cup, they boldly charged the hole on putts they would otherwise have lagged. They disregarded sidehill breaks on three-footers. Olin Dutra, who had the most beautiful putting touch I've ever seen, four-putted twice. Bill Mehlhorn three-putted 13 times! And irony had its day; Sarazen himself took three putts on seven greens.

I'm sure that many readers have similarly suffered at those times when it seemed practical to change tactics.

For instance, you may recall times in four-ball matches where your partner had already tied the hole, thus leaving you a free run on your putt for the win.

Knowing that you had everything to win and nothing to lose, your attitude toward your putt was, perhaps, "Whatever you do, dummy, don't leave it short."

Consequently, you struck the putt with a bit more verve than normal. And it may have rolled past the hole so fast that it would not have dropped, even if it had caught the cup dead-center. Or if it were a breaking putt, perhaps the ball's extra speed kept it from curving as much as you had anticipated.

"At least I gave it a chance," you may have said to yourself or your partner. But did you really? More likely it was your conscious effort to give it a chance, your departure from your normal putting tactics, that actually led to your missing.

Short putts. The "never-up, never-in" theory does apply to short putts. It's a must. But you should apply it all the time, on any putt you think you should hole. It should be a normal, built-in part of your putting strategy, not reserved just for those occasions where you have a free run, or when you must hole out to save the day.

Making it a firm policy to be aggressive on these putts not only assures your ball of reaching the target; the more aggressive roll of the ball also makes it less susceptible to the effects of spike marks and footprints around the cup.

How firmly should you stroke these putts? I suggest you visualize beforehand the ball entering the hole and then contacting the back side of the metal cup more or less halfway down. In your mind's eye, "see" it making the initial contact at this point, rather than barely toppling vertically downward to the bottom of the hole, or driving forward into the upper edge of the cup (see *Illustration 18*).

Normally I apply the never-up, never-in theory—and the image of the ball striking the back of the cup midway down—on putts up to 10 feet in length. I depart from this approach, however, if the green is especially fast, or if I'm putting downhill, or if I'm putting on extremely sidehill terrain. Then I might not apply this theory on a putt of even two or three feet.

For then I must consider the risk of three-putting if my ball should miss the hole. So I summon forth a different mental image. I visualize the ball toppling just over the front edge of the hole at a speed that will cause it to drop straight to the bottom of the cup.

Your personal outer limit for applying the never-up, never-in tactic might be eight feet or six feet. It all depends on your realistic assessment of your current putting skill.

As a general guideline, however, you should develop your skills to this extent: On any putt you think you should make, you should be able to reach or pass the hole 19 out of 20 times without ever three-putting.

Medium-length putts. These are somewhat longer putts where the never-up, never-in theory must be tempered. I'm not going to be terribly chagrined if I leave a 20-footer an inch or two short of the hole dead on line. If I let my temper rise on such occasions, I will soon be putting poorly, generally, perhaps three-putting from the far side all too frequently.

Depending on your skill, your combined goal on these putts might well be to reach the cup, say, 80 percent of the time without ever risking going so far past as to three-putt. Your image might well be that of having the ball contact the far-bottom side of the cup, rather than its far-middle portion, as shown in *Illustration 18*.

In determining your strategy on these putts, you should consider that in many instances it is better to make the second putt from beyond, rather than in front of, the cup. Doing so gives you the added advantage of having seen the reaction of the ball after it passed the hole on your first putt. This provides you with a fairly realistic impression of just how the second putt will break, if at all.

On normal putts on normal greens, your medium-range strategy might well apply to putts of 10 to 20 feet. Again, however, you must be prepared to forgo the never-up, never-in theory entirely on putts of less than 10 feet, whenever the slickness or terrain of the green makes going for even the bottom of the cup too risky.

Also, I do advocate that you grip the club a bit more firmly with both hands on putts that are near the outer limit of your medium range. This will allow you to putt the ball the necessary length while only increasing slightly the length of your stroke. With a slightly firmer grip you will need to make only a slightly longer stroke on a 20-footer than on a 10-footer, rather than a stroke of twice the length.

18. Proper distance control

You will find it simpler to make your putts go the proper distance if you imagine that the ball will contact the back-middle of the cup on short putts and the back-bottom of the cup on medium-length putts. On long putts, try to make the ball finish within an imaginary circle around the hole. Also, whenever possible, ask to have the flagstick attended on long putts. It will be an additional indicator of the putt's length.

Long putts. Only the foolhardy apply the never-up, never-in theory on long putts. On the rare occasions when I have tried to pass the hole on a putt of 30 feet or more, I have invariably three-putted. It's happened so often, it has become a phobia with me.

The challenge on longer putts, especially on those beyond 30 feet, is not to hole out, but to avoid three-putting. I suggest that on putts beyond your medium range you visualize a circle around the hole, as *Illustration 18* demonstrates. This circle may be three, four or even five feet wide, depending on your skill and the difficulty of the putt. Try to lag the putt so that the ball stops within that circle—any place therein.

This is the percentage approach. It will reduce your number of three-putt greens.

In fact, most people who putt for a circle find they actually sink *more* long putts than they did when putting for the hole itself. I strongly suspect this happens because lagging for the circle makes a golfer more distance-conscious. Going for the cup tends to make him too direction-oriented.

Direction is important on all putts, but as the length increases, proper distance becomes more and more the priority. The vast majority of three-putts results from the first putt finishing too long or too short, rather than too far left or right.

I suggest a still firmer grip pressure on long putts. This will make the ball roll the longer distance without your lengthening your stroke so much that it becomes too difficult to contact the ball solidly. Misconnecting with the ball becomes more and more penal as the length of putts increases.

Finally, on all long putts, and even on medium-length putts, I suggest that you ask to have the flagstick attended, even if you do not need that aid to see the hole. The flagstick and the person holding it then become additional aids in helping you sense how far it is to the hole.

Reading greens. There are certain things eyes can and cannot do. When it comes to reading greens and visualizing the proper line to the hole, the eyes function best when the view is binocular—when you view the upcoming putt from behind the ball with both your eyes as level as possible and low to the ground. Crouch down. I have never seen a

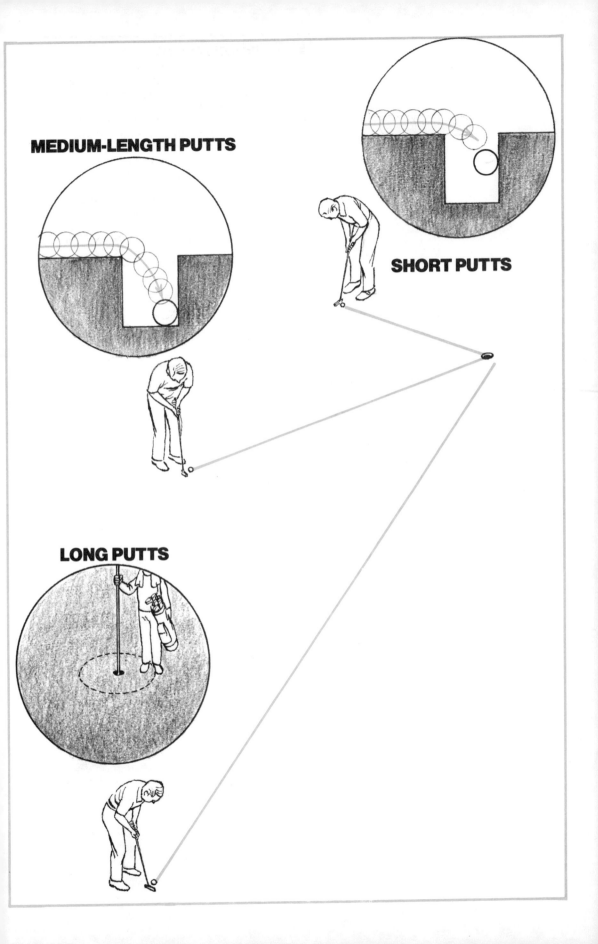

MEDIUM-LENGTH PUTTS

SHORT PUTTS

LONG PUTTS

19. Reading greens

Though you might view putts from the side to gain an overall impression, you should determine your specific putting line from behind the ball, crouching down low with your eyes level. Visualize the entire trip the ball will take to the hole, then look for slight blemishes or discolorations in the grass that are on or near that route. These reference points can reinforce your ability to aim correctly, especially if one of them is on your line and within a foot or so of your ball. Aim the club at this intermediate target, rather than the hole itself. Once you have aimed the putter and positioned yourself, you have done all you can about direction. Thereafter, concentrate solely on making the ball roll the correct distance at a speed which will allow it to hold the line you have chosen.

good putter who did not determine his or her specific putting line from this low, behind-the-ball perspective.

I do think it is advantageous to first look at putts from the side, standing midway between the ball and the hole, so long as you do not delay play in doing so. This view provides a valuable impression of the putt's overall length and any uphill or downhill terrain it will need to pass over. However, the final selection of the putting line should be made from behind the ball.

I suggest you follow the lead of Mickey Wright, the all-time great woman professional. Mickey has said that she did her best putting when she visualized the entire trip that the ball would take to the hole as well as its successful entry into the cup (see *illustration 19*).

See the entire line. In fact, you should see not only that line, but also any imperfections in the green that might be on it or close alongside it. Nothing gives me more confidence than to have two or three such reference points along the way. There might be, say, a specific spike mark on the line a foot or so in front of the ball, a small discoloration in the green farther down the line or a repaired ball mark beyond that.

These reference points are what we call intermediate targets. The most important of these, however, is one that occurs within a foot or so of where your ball rests—one that is directly on your intended line, as shown in *Illustration 19*. This close-in reference point greatly helps you aim on line much more reliably than does the distant hole itself.

In short, determine the line from behind the ball, pick a spot on or near that line within a foot of the ball, grip the putter correctly and aim it with reference to that spot. Then adjust yourself into your final address position.

At this point, you have done all you can as far as direction is concerned. Thereafter, length becomes your primary focus. Before and during your stroke you should concentrate merely on rolling the ball with enough speed to hold the line and finish according to your pre-putt strategy, whether it be to contact the mid-back of the cup (on a short putt), the bottom-back (on a medium putt) or to finish within your imaginary circle (on long putts).

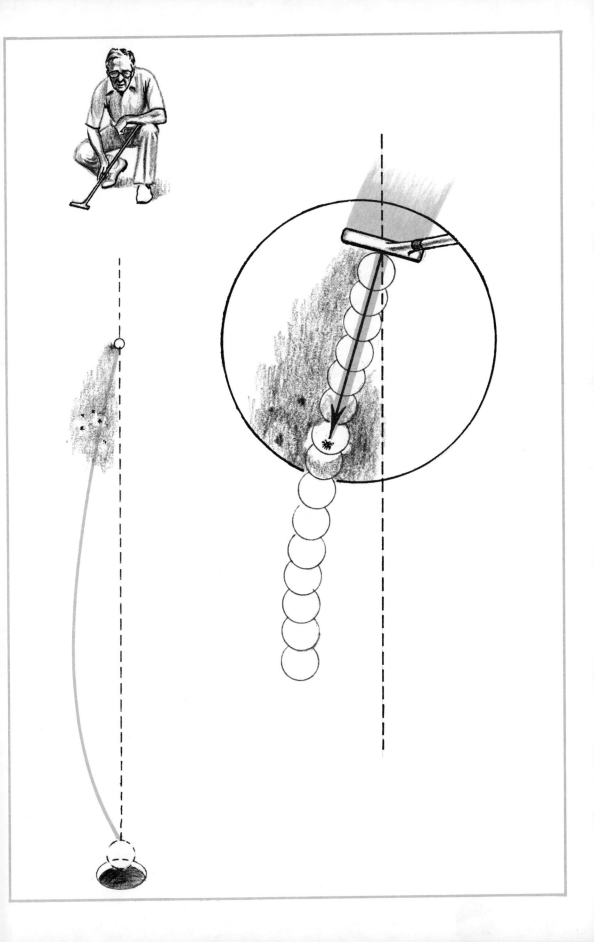

I should alert you at this point to something that you might experience when you first adopt the practice of aiming your putter at an intermediate target in front of the ball. You may find that an intermediate target, which was obviously on your putting line when your view was from behind the ball, appears to be to the left or right of that overall line once you set yourself to the side of the ball.

This is not unusual. Our eyes tend to give us a different visual message when they view something from a different perspective. This phenomenon is no doubt a major reason why so many golfers, perhaps most, do fail to aim the putter down their chosen line.

Again, however, your most reliable perspective is the binocular view from behind the ball. If you choose an intermediate target that is on your chosen line, as viewed from behind the ball, you must aim the putter at that target to remain on that line.

Obviously, it will take some courage to putt over an intermediate target that appears to be off line when you finally set yourself into putting position, even though Paul Runyan tells you you should.

All I can say is that you must persist. You must learn to aim correctly. You must train your eyes to see the same putting line when you are over the ball that you saw, correctly, from behind the ball.

It may take a few practice sessions to do this retraining of your eyes. So be it. If you do not learn to aim correctly, you will inevitably develop a compensatory stroke to make the ball roll on line even though you have aimed off line. You will not be a consistently excellent putter with such a stroke.

As you practice, continue to choose an intermediate target from behind the ball and to aim accordingly. If at first your putts tend to finish consistently either left or right of target, it will be because you had, in the past, developed an incorrect stroke to compensate for your tendency to misaim. Now that you are aiming correctly, such a stroke will make you miss putts for a time. Soon, however, your natural instincts will take over. If you continue to aim correctly, your stroke will become correct, simply as a result of your trying to sink the putt. At that point, you will be aiming correctly and stroking correctly, instead of misaiming and stroking incorrectly. Your reward will be more putts dropped.

There is no escaping the fact that learning to read greens takes experience. But here are a few things you should consider to make your learning occur faster and more effectively.

—How long is the grass on the green? The longer the grass is, the faster the ball must roll to reach the hole. This additional speed of roll will reduce the influence of any sidehill terrain on the path of the putt. In short, the longer the grass, the less the putt will break.

—How wide are the blades of the grass? Thick-bladed grasses, such as Bermuda strains, tend to make greens slower than do the thin-bladed bent grasses. The ball must roll faster on such greens to reach the hole. Thus, sidehill putts on thick-bladed grasses do not curve as much as they do on thin-bladed grasses.

—Are you putting uphill or downhill? Uphill putts must roll faster, downhill putts slower, to finish at or just beyond the hole. Since faster-rolling putts are less affected by sidehill terrain, upslope sidehillers will break less than will downslope sidehillers.

—What is the terrain around the hole? During the latter stages of a putt, when the ball is slowing down, gravity has its greatest effect. Be particularly cognizant of any sidehill terrain near the cup.

—Is there a strong wind blowing? Yes, strong wind *will* affect the direction a putt rolls. You must allow for that influence, moreso if the greens are cut especially short and/or the grass is narrow-bladed. Both of these factors reduce the amount of friction between the ball and the green, thus allowing the wind to have more effect.

—Is there any grain? Grain is grass that lies flat in a consistent direction. The ball will curve in that direction, unless offset by terrain sloping in the opposite direction. Downgrain putts will run farther than normal. Putting into the grain reduces length.

Patches or areas of a green that appear lighter or darker than their surroundings usually indicate grain is present. Grainy grass appears lighter than normal, almost silvery, when it is running away from you; it appears dark green when running toward you.

Grain will often grow in the same direction that the prevailing wind blows. Also, it will tend to grow in the direction that the sun sets. Thus, in Florida, where the sun sets in the west and the winds blow to the northwest, I've always found that grain grows a bit toward west of northwest.

Choosing A Putter

To be a true artist on the greens, you should be as selective in choosing a putter as, say, a master violinist would be in choosing his or her instrument. Once you do find a good putter, I hope you will stick with it. Changing from putter to putter forces you to similarly alter your technique, fitting it to whatever implement you happen to be using at the time. This continual varying of style is not conducive to consistently excellent putting results over the long haul.

Length. Your first consideration—though not necessarily your most important—is the putter's overall length. The length that is right for you will depend primarily on your height *and* the length of your arms.

Usually, tall people have relatively long arms, short people relatively short arms. Therefore, the actual distance from the hands to the ground, which is the meaningful factor in determining putter length, will not be all that different between a six-foot man and a five-foot woman. The difference might well be just two or three inches, rather than the entire 12-inch difference in their overall heights.

Generally, a tall man whose arms are of normal length for his stature, would do well with a 37-inch putter. A person in the 5 foot-6 inch to 6-foot range, again with arms of normal length, might well use a 36-inch putter. Shorter men and women should probably seek one in the 34-35 inch range.

However, if your arms are unusually long, you would want to consider a somewhat shorter putter than I have just suggested for a person of your height. If they are unusually short for a person of your height, you would probably need a longer shaft.

To find the exact length of putter for you, I suggest you hold the one you are considering one-half to three-quarters of an inch from the end and sole it lightly on the floor or the ground.

Make sure that you grip the club with each palm facing inward and upward at the 45-degree angle I mentioned earlier in this section. Make sure that you bend comfortably at the knees and hips so that your eyes are over the putting line. Also, rest your upper arms lightly against your rib cage with your forearms directly in front of and behind the imaginary shaft extension.

If, when you adopt this model address position, you find that your forearms do angle into the shaft at 45-degree angles, the putter in your hand is the proper length for you. However, if these angles are less than 45 degrees, your hands are too low and the putter is too short. It is too long for you if it forces your hands to be so high that the angles are greater than 45 degrees.

Effective lie. Closely allied with a putter's length is its effective lie. Both factors have much to do with how far away from the putting line the club forces you to stand.

In clubs other than putters, the "lie" is the angle at which the shaft enters the clubhead. Specifically, it is the angle measured between the underside (your side) of the shaft and the ground when the clubhead is soled.

In the case of putters, however, the rules allow the shaft to be curved or bent. Thus, it is more realistic to consider the "effective lie" of the putter as being the degree that the upward extension of the shaft departs from being vertical when the club is soled flat on a level surface.

This departure from vertical, according to the rules, must be at least 10 degrees. Thus, whenever you sole a legal putter flat on a horizontal surface, the shaft must angle upward somewhat toward you. This sets your hands a bit to your side of the putting line. The more the upward angling of the shaft departs from vertical—the "flatter" the club's effective lie—the farther inside the line your hands will tend to be.

In short, a putter with an extremely flat effective lie can force you to stand too far from the putting line when you sole the head flat on a horizontal surface. An extremely "upright" putter, with the shaft perhaps extending upward at the minimal, 10-degree departure from vertical, might well make you stand too close to the ball.

Once you have found a putter with the correct length for you, it becomes important that it also have the correct effective lie. That lie will be correct if you can (1) assume the prescribed grip—again, make sure you hold it one-half to three-quarter inches from the top end, (2) bend comfortably from the knees and hips with (3) the imaginary shaft extending upward between your forearms—not above or below either, (4) lightly sole the club flat on a level surface and (5) still find that your eyes are over the line.

If you assume these positions and find that your eyes are set over an area on your side of the line, then the effective lie of the putter is too flat for you. If your eyes set out beyond the line, the putter's effective lie is too upright.

Generally speaking, I feel that most golfers would do better with putters that tend toward the upright. This is based on my earlier observation that most golfers tend to address putts with their eyes positioned to the inside of their putting line, a problem that is aggravated by putters with effective lies that are relatively flat.

Weight. I believe that most people should use a medium to heavy putter. The exception would be persons who are very slight and delicate, especially some women. For these, I advocate a medium to light weight. Certainly heavy-handed people, whose hands and wrists are strong, should use a medium or heavy putter, heavy in most cases.

There is a belief that golfers who usually play on courses with lightning-fast greens should use light putters. I disagree. It is all too easy to move a light putter too fast. Within certain limits, clubhead speed is more a factor than clubhead mass in providing distance. Thus a fast-moving putter, even though light, can be murderous on slick greens. This is especially true if it also has a whippy shaft.

In short, my vote goes to the medium to heavy putter regardless of the greens' speed. Its heavier mass provides sufficient momentum on slow greens and its tendency to move slower makes distance control easier on slick greens.

Shaft flex. The amount that a shaft flexes as you stroke the putt depends on its length and how the club's overall weight is distributed. All things being equal, a longer shaft will flex or bend more than a shorter shaft. A putter with a light shaft and a heavy head will bend more than one with a heavy shaft and a light head.

If the shaft is poker stiff, you will not be able to feel the putterhead at all. This might affect your sense of touch somewhat, making it more difficult to control distance.

However, a shaft that is too whippy will make distance control even harder. At times the clubhead will whip into the ball, which then will slingshot off the face. Also, a whippy shaft will tend to twist more than a stiff shaft. This makes clubface alignment—direction—also more difficult to control.

Thus, I suggest you look for a putter that does not give you any feeling of shaft bend as you stroke long putts. The actual classification of the shaft, whether it be medium flex or stiff, is immaterial in itself. What is important to you is how it feels when you swing it. Hopefully, it will feel relatively firm.

Putterhead balance. I personally feel that putterhead balance is a vital consideration in choosing a putter. I say this because it determines in large part your ability to square the putterface to your line time after time, without having to manipulate the club unnaturally with your hands.

You can test a putter's balance by simply laying the clubshaft across the top of your extended forefinger. Position your finger under the shaft at whatever point you must for the club to hold steady in a horizontal position.

Then check to see how the putterhead is positioned. If the head is horizontal, so that the face looks either directly upward or downward, your putter has the best possible balance, in my opinion.

Few putters, however, have such exceptional balance. Most will hang with putterhead vertical, the toe pointing straight downward. This type of balance is acceptable, if not ideal, for squaring the face to the line consistently.

I would avoid using a putter if the head hangs aslant, somewhere between vertical and horizontal. I have found that this sort of balance is least reliable for making putts consistently roll in the right direction (*see Illustration 20*).

Face depth and loft. The distance from the top to the bottom of the putterface is its depth. The degree that the face looks upward when the shaft is perpendicular—tilted neither left nor right—is its loft. Depth and loft combine to help determine how the ball will take off from the putterface.

Almost all putters have some loft, even if just a degree or two. This slight upward facing, ideally, lifts the ball infinitesimally, just enough to get it out of its resting spot and up onto the top of the grass.

Also, the slight loft provides a margin of safety in case contact occurs with the top of the clubshaft a bit in lead of the head. In such cases, if the face had no built-in loft, it would actually be looking slightly downward at contact. The club would then pinch the ball downward into the green, causing an unreliable skidding and bouncing action.

The depth of the putterface also affects how the putt will start out. A putter with a shallow depth of face will tend to make the ball start out higher, with a deep-face lower. Thus, the combinations to be wary of in putters are (1) shallow faces combined with an exceptional amount of loft, which can make the ball take off too high, and (2) deep faces with too little loft, which can drive the ball downward into the green.

Most certainly you would not want a deep-faced putter with minimal loft, if your tendency is to contact putts with your hands leading the putterhead.

To find the right combination of face depth and loft for you, I suggest you actually putt on a level part of the practice green with the putters you are considering. Set up to putt with the ball positioned opposite your left big toe, as I have suggested, so contact occurs when the putterhead is moving level with the ground, neither downward nor upward. Also, address the putt with your puttershaft perpendicular, tilted neither to your left or right.

Stroke putts, and notice what the ball does when it comes off the putterface on those tries in which you do make solid contact. I would avoid buying a putter that noticeably lofts the ball into the air or one that causes it to skid in the grass before it starts to roll freely forward.

Sole line. The sole, or bottom, of any putter you choose should have some degree of curvature, so the toe and heel ends are slightly off the ground when the club is soled flat on a level surface. A dead-straight sole line makes it too easy for the toe or heel of the putterhead to scrape,

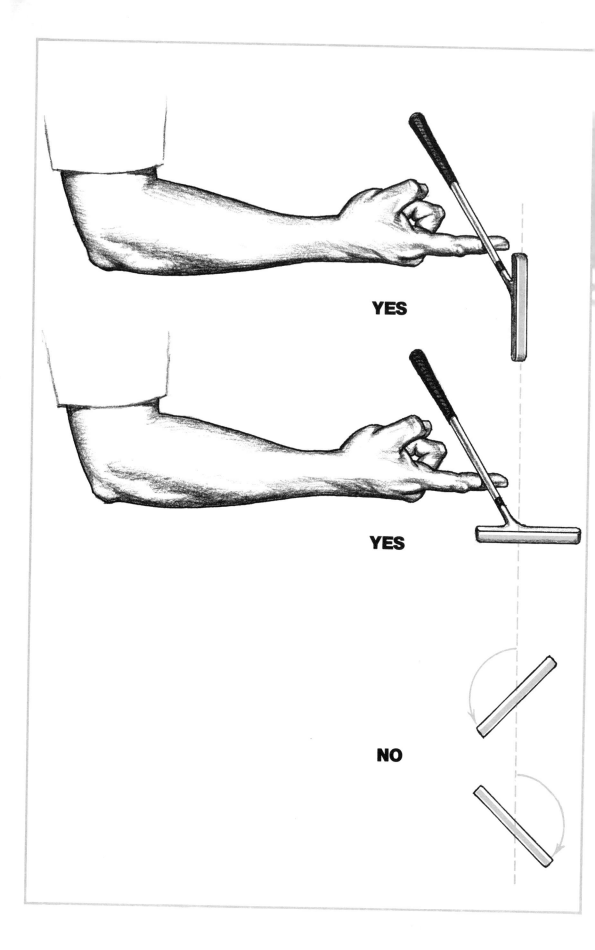

YES

YES

NO

20. Putterhead balance

By balancing a putter across your forefinger, as shown here, you can note the positioning that the putterhead adopts and determine how well it is balanced. A well-balanced putterhead is easier to square to your putting line at contact without manipulating the club unnaturally with your hands. I believe that the putterhead which hangs vertically (top drawing) is acceptable. A rare find is one that is so well balanced that it hangs horizontally. I would avoid those than hang somewhere in between vertical and horizontal when this test is applied.

or dig into, the grass.

There are putters available today which have extremely curved soles; they look like the rockers on rocking chairs. These putters do eliminate digging with the toe or heel; however, the sole, being so extremely curved, does not offer a great deal of guidance as to what part should actually rest on the green. It becomes all too easy to stand too far away from the line, by resting the sole toward its heel end, or too close to the line by setting the club toward the toe end of the sole. This is not an insurmountable problem, but those who use such putters must continually check to see that their eyes are over the putting line.

Blade vs. mallet. Deciding between a putter with a "blade" head or a "mallet" head is largely a matter of personal preference. However, I do feel it is important, in either case, to select a putter with a head that is easy to aim.

I personally find it easy to aim a blade putter, because its trailing side runs straight and parallel with the face itself. This gives me two straight lines to set square to my initial putting line. The back edge of most mallet-headed putters, of course, is rounded, thus disallowing this symmetrical advantage.

However, there are some mallet putters that feature two or more parallel lines running across the top of the head. These lines do aid greatly in aiming, if the golfer trains himself to set them parallel to his putting line. Some putters, in fact, have these lines spaced across the top of the head so the outermost and innermost lines are exactly one ball-width apart. This provides an excellent guide in that if you address every putt with these lines bracketing the ball, your chances of contacting it consistently on the same spot of the putterface are greatly enhanced.

Sweet spot. Having just mentioned the use of lines across the top of the putter, this is a good time to talk about the "sweet spot." Too often the line or lines across the top of a putter, while helpful in aiming, are misleading in terms of where you should address the ball on the putterface.

Every putter has a sweet spot, that being the spot on the face where

21. Finding the sweet spot

To make your putts consistently roll the right distance, it is vital to contact the ball directly on the "sweet spot." Missing this spot by only a fraction of an inch can make a putt of, say, 20 feet finish two or three feet short. To find your putter's sweet spot, hold the end of the shaft gently between your thumb and forefinger, as shown here. With a golf tee or pencil in the other hand, tap across the face of the putter. Tapping toward the toe or heel end of the face will make the putter twist. As your tapping nears the sweet spot, the putterhead will begin to rebound straight back, where the putterhead does not twist. Your sweet spot will be in the middle of that area. Address all putts with the ball directly opposite that spot.

contact with the ball is most solid. Tests have shown that contact made on that spot will send the ball farther and straighter than will contact made even one-fourth inch or more off that spot. Missing the sweet spot by a mere half inch, as golfers frequently do, will make the putt come up some 10 to 15 percent shorter and 5 to 10 percent off line.

In most putters, the sweet spot is not in the center of the face, but somewhere between face-center and the heel. Thus, golfers who try to contact putts on face-center do themselves a disservice. If they succeed in their efforts, contact occurs to the toe side of the sweet spot. The ball does not roll as far as it should and it tends to roll off to the right.

The problem is heightened by the fact that many manufacturers who put a guideline or two across the top of the putterhead set them at or near its center, or outside the sweet spot. Since golfers tend to address putts with these lines directly behind the back side of the ball, they all but insure less-than-solid contact on most putts.

I suggest you find the actual sweet spot on your putter. Then file a line across the top of the head to indicate where it is, so you can address all putts opposite that line. This is something I frequently do for my club members if the putters they have or buy lack such guidelines, or if the guidelines are far from the actual sweet spot.

To find the sweet spot on your putter, merely dangle it from the grip end with your thumb and forefinger, so the entire shaft hangs freely. Then lift the club and tap the face with a pointed object, such as a golf tee or a ball-point pen, that you are holding in your other hand. Tap across the face of the club. You will find that when you tap toward the toe or heel, the clubface will want to twist open or closed. As you tap nearer and nearer the sweet spot, this twisting will decrease. You will find that there is a small area on the face, perhaps a half-inch to an inch in width, wherein the tapping causes no twisting whatsoever. Your sweet spot will be in the middle of that area (see *Illustration 21*).

Center-shafted vs. heel-shafted putters. In most cases, the sweet spot on heel-shafted putters is more toward the heel than it is in the so-called center-shafted putters. Also, many times, the center-shafted putter seems to have a wider area on each side of the sweet

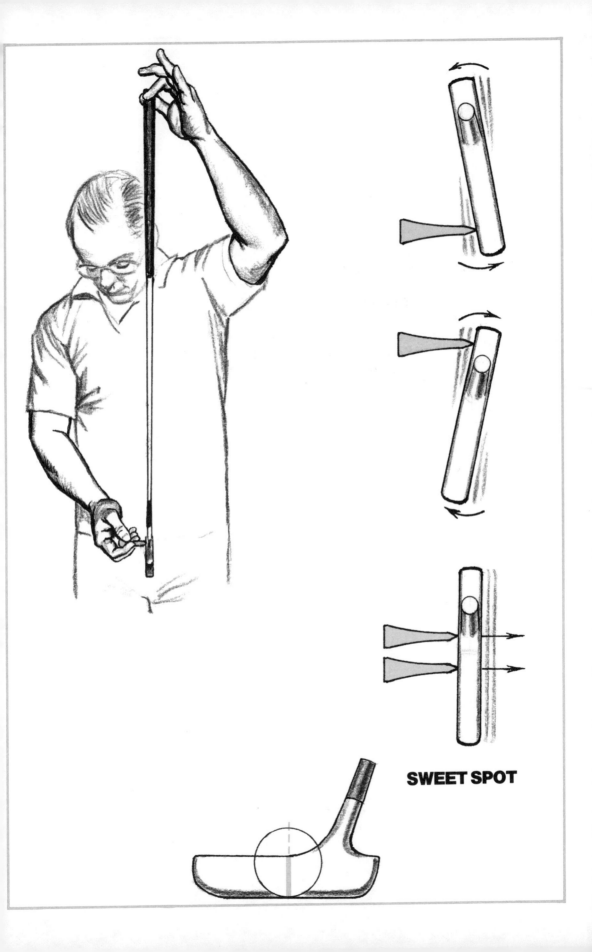

SWEET SPOT

spot wherein you can still make fairly solid contact. For these reasons, I tend to prefer the center-shafted variety.

I must point out, however, that there are many heel-shafted putters that do have the effect of being center-shafted. These are putters with curved or bent shafts in which the top part, the grip portion—if extended to the head on a continuous straight line—would enter well outward from the heel. These putters are fine so long as the bend or curve of the shaft is not so extreme that it forces you to stand too far from the ball when the clubhead is soled.

The grip. The putter's gripping material should be tacky enough so your hands can adhere to it without your having to squeeze the life out of the club before or during your stroke.

Also, I personally prefer that the shape of the grip not be cylindrical. It helps guide the golfer to position the hands and aim the club the same way from putt to putt if the gripping portion of the shaft is flat on top.

Finally, I suggest you avoid grips that seem a bit thin in overall diameter. You will find that a thicker grip encourages a firm-wristed stroke made with the forearms, rather than a wristy stroke with the hands.

SECTION 3: CHIPPING

     You are playing the 18th hole of an important match that is tied. You and your opponent have played the same number of strokes on that hole. As you approach the green, which is fairly level, you see the two balls. They appear to be the same distance from the hole, say, 30 feet. But one ball is actually on the putting surface and the other is about six feet off the edge.

     Which of those balls do you hope is yours?

     If you are like most golfers, I suspect you hope that the ball already on the green is yours. Given the option, you would probably much rather putt than chip, for almost all golfers find it easier to make the ball finish in or near the hole on a putt than they do on a chip shot of the same length.

     One reason is that solid contact comes easier on putts. The lesser loft of the putter over a chipping club makes it simpler to contact the back of the ball without the club stubbing into the ground. Another reason is that the ball usually sets up better on the green than it does in the longer grass around it. Also, the putt does not fly through the air an appreciable amount and thus is less likely than the chip to bounce off line upon landing. Finally, since most golfers tend to practice their putting more than their chipping, they have developed more skill in that area.

     These are all valid reasons why golfers prefer putting to chipping. There are still other explanations, however, which indicate why my chipping technique is superior to other, more orthodox methods.

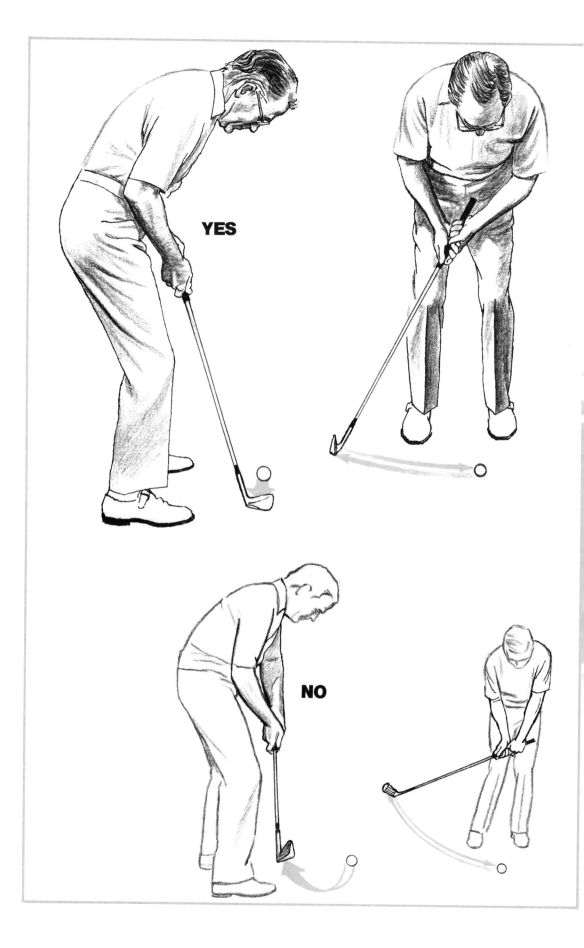

22. Chip like you putt

You will derive several advantages on chip shots if you play them with the same address position—eyes over the line—same grip and same wristless stroke that I advocate for putting (upper drawings), rather than the more conventional method (lower drawings) which allows the wrists to hinge. The clubhead moves back and forward more or less along the line for a longer duration with less opening and closing of the clubface. This improves directional accuracy. The wrist-free stroke is simpler, so solid contact is more likely. It also eliminates the additional speed producer—the wrists—for better distance control. It minimizes backspin to create a truer bounce and roll of the ball.

For instance, if you study other golfers, you will usually see differences between the way they putt and the way they chip. A common difference is that the player stands farther away from the ball when chipping. It is equally as common to find that he applies more wrist action—more cocking and uncocking—when chipping than putting.

Were that player to use the same grip chipping that he uses when putting, were he to set up to his chip shot in almost the same way he sets up to putt and were he to make the same stroke chipping as he does when putting, his chipping skill would become more in line with his putting proficiency (see Illustration 22).

Moreover, if that golfer were to chip as he putts, any improvement that he made in his putting—as hopefully you will after adopting my putting methods—would also, automatically, cause a similar improvement in chipping.

In short, you will find that the things I advise for chipping are in large part the same things I advise for putting. I hope you will become a better putter because of my putting instruction and your dedication to mastering it. I also hope that, through similar implementation of the same methodology, you will improve your chipping to an even greater extent. Ideally, you will improve your chipping to the point that it makes no difference whether your ball is on the green or off the green a similar distance from the hole.

Chipping Technique

Though I've added a few refinements over the past five decades, I developed my basic chipping style during a six- to eight-month period back in my caddying days. As is usually the case with golfers, the conditions under which I learned the game dictated my style of play.

The Hot Springs (Ark.) Golf and Country Club where I worked had sand greens. The putting surface was a very thin layer of sand spread over a base of firm Arkansas clay. This clay base had various small depressions in it which would fill with sand when the green was dragged smooth. Thus, while the sand layer over most of the green was just the merest fraction of an inch in depth, it could be as much as two inches deep over these depressions in the underlying clay.

If your approach shot happened to land in one of these pockets, the ball would dig deep into the sand before bouncing forward. It was almost like landing in one of our modern bunkers. The ball would finish far short of the hole. Sometimes it would kick off line.

A ball that landed short of the green often reacted similarly. The coarse Bermuda grass would grab the ball or knock it sideways. Because the greens were only 60 to 75 feet across, there were many times when you did need to land the ball short in this unpredictable turf.

Both the sand pockets on the green and the Bermuda grass around it were particularly damning to high shots that had relatively little forward momentum. I also found that shots carrying a large degree of backspin dug still deeper into the sand or the grass. Height and spin were things to be avoided as much as possible on chip shots.

I needed a chip shot that would readily "walk through" the sand on the green or the grass around it. I needed a low-flying shot that would land with a minimum of bite and then bounce and roll freely forward without kicking off to the side.

The first thing I did to keep my shots low was to chip with clubs that had fewer degrees of built-in loft. Whenever possible, I chose the least-lofted club that would land the ball on the green and still make it stop before running well past the hole. Instead of playing a high-flying 9-iron to land well onto the green, I might choose a 5-iron—then called a mashie—to land just over the edge.

These lower shots bounded forward more readily, even if they landed in a sand pocket or the Bermuda grass. The lesser loft also reduced the amount of spin applied to the ball to some extent, because straighter-faced clubs make contact a bit higher on the ball, less on its underside.

However, I still needed some way to reduce backspin, especially when the situation called for a chip with a more-lofted club.

I finally found a way to make the ball fly practically spin-free, like a knuckleball pitch in baseball, at least with any club up to an 8-iron or 9-iron. Today, if you watched me chip a driving-range ball with a stripe around its equator, you would see that the stripe makes no more than two or three revolutions while the ball is in flight. Such a shot creates little, if any, depression upon landing, simply because reducing spin eliminates much of the friction created between the ball and the surface on which it lands.

I learned to play chip shots that were relatively free of spin by holding the club with a putting grip and taking all wrist action out of my stroke. This stroke, with the arms moving freely from the shoulder joints, provides other advantages in chipping that go beyond merely decreasing the ball's spin.

For instance, any time you add wrist action to your swing, you add an additional speed producer, an element that makes the clubhead move faster. Thus, you add something that requires additional control to make the shot go the right distance.

Actually, wrist action not only adds speed to the clubhead, it also makes it go too fast too quickly. It is this increased *rate* of acceleration that really makes the clubhead's speed more difficult to control. It makes the ball come off the clubface too "hot," as we say.

Without wrist action, with only the slower-moving arms in motion, the clubhead's speed increases more gradually. This makes distance much more controllable, more predictable. You can still swing your arms a bit too fast, and the ball will finish a bit too far past the hole. However, the result will be far less disastrous than if the wrists are also allowed to contribute additional acceleration.

Wrist action also complicates the matter of making solid contact. When the wrists hinge during the backstroke, they make the clubhead come up higher off the ground than it would with an arms-only stroke. To return that clubhead to ball-level at contact, the wrists must then unhinge more or less the same degree.

They must also unhinge the same amount for the club to be carrying the right degree of effective loft at contact. If they unhinge too late, the club's effective loft will be too slight; the shot will fly too low. It will either land short of where you had planned it should, perhaps short of the green, or it will land where you had planned, but will run too far.

If the wrists unhinge too early, the club will be carrying more loft than you had planned for by the time it finally gets to the ball. Given solid contact, the ball will fly higher than you had expected. It will often settle too quickly, well short of the hole. Sometimes it will spin off to the right upon landing.

Frequently, unhinging the wrists too soon not only leaves the club facing too much upward at contact, but also finds it *moving* upward as well. Then the sharp, leading edge of the clubface makes contact high on the ball and line-drives it too low and too far.

On short shots we do not need the extra distance and spin that wrist action provides. The firm-wristed, arms-only stroke is far more reliable for making solid contact with the clubhead moving at the right speed and carrying the right degree of effective loft. It allows the ball to fly with less spin, which creates a truer bounce upon landing, and is certainly more reliable under pressure, when those quick-reacting wrist joints can let you down.

Moreover, using the putting grip and address positions that are so vital in producing the firm-wristed stroke will greatly improve your directional accuracy on chip shots.

Despite all of these advantages, I must confess that the bane of my existence as an instructor has been my inability to convince expert golfers to practice what I preach for chipping. It is important that you understand why these players resist the change because you, too, may experience some difficulty at first.

Specifically, you may find that eliminating wrist action from your chipping stroke reduces the shot's distance. This is normal and understandable; by eliminating wrist action you take away something that produced additional clubhead speed.

It does not take a great deal of time and effort to adjust your sense of touch to allow for this loss of length. And I believe that the advantages of the wrist-free stroke far outweigh this temporary setback. Of course, the professional golfer is understandably more resistant to changing his technique. In most cases, he already chips fairly well with the style he has used for years. Also, even a temporary loss of distance control can mean a substantial loss of earnings for the more successful competitor.

I do see more and more touring pros employing a wrist-free chipping stroke every year, and I'm sure it will become even more popular in the future. Perhaps some day even Jack Nicklaus, whom I think chips like an 8–10 handicapper, will gravitate toward using less wrist action. I sometimes wonder how many more tournaments Jack would have won, given his otherwise incomparable game and emotional attitude, had he acquired a really fine chipping technique as we are describing here.

The firm-wristed chipping stroke. Now let's spell out precisely how to make the firm-wristed chipping stroke. First, let me mention the things in chipping that are the same as in putting.

As demonstrated in *Illustration 23,* hold the club with both palms facing inward and upward halfway between vertical and horizontal—45 degrees. Hold the club with equally firm pressure in each hand. Maintain this same pressure throughout the stroke—no relaxing, no grabbing—and hold the club at address so that only a small fraction of its weight sets on the grass.

The arms should be positioned as in putting, with each forearm approaching the clubshaft at a 45-degree angle. The club itself should be angled so the shaft, if extended upward, would run parallel to your forearms. We want the arms in position to apply force directly to the shaft as you push and pull it on the proper path during the stroke. Your upper arms should rest lightly against your rib cage.

Set your feet so both point directly forward, at right angles to your target line. Neither should be turned outward or inward to the left or the right. And, your toes should be an equal distance from your target line, so an imaginary line across them would run parallel to that line.

So far everything I've said about chipping technique is identical to putting. Here are two things you may need to vary slightly, though.

In putting, I stressed that your eyes should set directly over your line, so that when you dangled the putter from the bridge of your nose it would cover that part of the line that extends from the back of the ball. This eye positioning is ideal for two reasons. First, it gives you your best possible perspective of the line when you are standing to the side of the ball. Thus, it helps you aim the putter in the right direction. Second, to set your eyes over the line, you must stand fairly close to the ball, if your other pre-stroke positions are correct. This proximity to your line makes it possible to stroke pretty much along that line. Only on medium to long putts does your putterhead move noticeably to the inside during your backstroke.

If you were to stand farther from the ball, with your eyes set well inside your line, your putter would move more to the inside during your backswing if you made a natural stroke. As a result, it would not be moving on line and facing down the line for as long a duration as it moved into the ball. In short, the farther you stood from a shot, the less your chances would become that your clubhead would move and face in the right direction at contact.

In chipping, as in putting, I still recommend that you set your eyes over the line. However, when chipping you will be using clubs that are longer than your putter. Also, the angle at which the shaft enters the head on these clubs is less upright than on most putters. These two factors combine to make most golfers stand too far from the line when chipping. If they also hold the club with their normal full-swing grip, this tendency to stand too far away from their work is further increased.

To get your eyes over the line with these longer, less upright clubs, you will need to grip farther down on the shaft than you do on your putter.

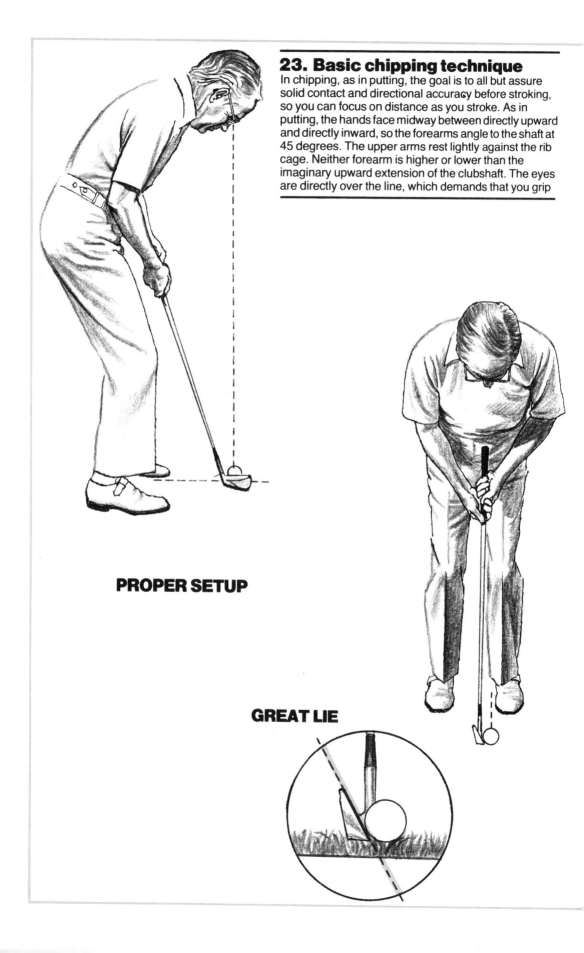

23. Basic chipping technique

In chipping, as in putting, the goal is to all but assure solid contact and directional accuracy before stroking, so you can focus on distance as you stroke. As in putting, the hands face midway between directly upward and directly inward, so the forearms angle to the shaft at 45 degrees. The upper arms rest lightly against the rib cage. Neither forearm is higher or lower than the imaginary upward extension of the clubshaft. The eyes are directly over the line, which demands that you grip

PROPER SETUP

GREAT LIE

well down on the club and, perhaps, set it lightly on the ground toward the toe end of the sole. On great lies, the ball is positioned a bit farther back to the right than on putts, but the weight is still evenly distributed between the feet. The worse the lie, the more weight you must set on your left foot—lean to the left—and the farther back to the right you must play the ball. The more you lean to the left and play the ball back to the right, the more-lofted club you will need to select to achieve a given height on the shot.

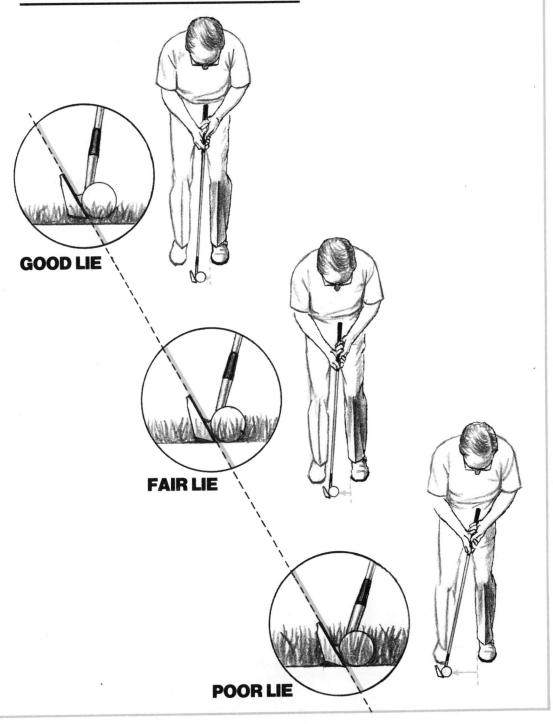

GOOD LIE

FAIR LIE

POOR LIE

To stand the same distance from the line on chip shots as on putts, you may need to grip so far down the shaft that your bottom hand is actually on the metal. So be it. At first this may feel strange, but it will begin to feel natural after one or two practice sessions.

By gripping down on the shaft, you will be shortening the length of your chipping club. This will make your shots travel a shorter distance than they have in the past, if you have been holding the club near the end and, as a result, standing farther from the ball.

Again, however, it will not take long for you to adjust your chipping touch to this loss of length. In the end, you will make better contact with the ball more frequently, because gripping down gives you better control over the club. Moreover, with your eyes set over the line, your directional control will improve dramatically.

I hope you will periodically dangle the chipping club from your nose to make sure you are setting your eyes over the line. You may be surprised at how close you must stand to the line. In fact, you may find that you will need to set the bottom of the club toward its toe end. Don't let this bother you. Do it. Take a chance. The eyes *must* be over the line for you to benefit fully. Remember, your goal is to give yourself every possible advantage for maximum directional accuracy *before* making the stroke, so you can focus solely on distance control *during* the stroke.

There is only one other change needed for chipping, because while on the putting surface itself the ball sets atop the grass, on most chip shots the ball nestles into the deeper grass around the green.

In putting, I suggested that you play the ball opposite the big toe of your left foot (right foot for left-handers). When chipping from an excellent lie where the ball sets up on the grass, play the ball just slightly farther back—to the right—in your stance. This slight modification will help assure that you contact the ball solidly without first stubbing the club in the grass behind it.

When the lie is slightly less than ideal, you will need to pinch the ball a little to insure solid contact. Position it as you did for a good lie, but also lean to the left at address. Put more weight onto your left foot than your right. This moves your suspension point to the left and further guarantees that you will contact the ball before you contact the turf.

If you have a bad lie, you will again need to lean left, but also play the ball still farther back to the right in your stance. The goal, remember, is to contact the ball before the turf.

In short, the worse the lie, the more you must pinch the shot. You increase your degree of pinch by leaning left and, perhaps, playing the ball farther back, more opposite stance-center or even your right foot (*see Illustration 23*).

Remember that the more you pinch the shot, the lower the ball will fly. The club will be descending at a sharper downward angle and thus the clubface will be carrying less effective loft. When pinching a shot, you will need a more-lofted club to achieve a given trajectory. The more the pinch, the more the built-in loft needed. A severely pinched 8-iron might fly like a 5-iron or a 6-iron. Therefore, to achieve an 8-iron trajectory, you might need a pitching wedge or a sand wedge in hand.

To summarize, you should play your chip shots just as you putt, except for (1) choking farther down on the club (so as to get your eyes over the line), and (2) leaning left with the ball on fair lies—leaning left with the ball still farther back on poorer lies.

You should read the green and visualize the shot just as you do when you putt. You should actually think that you are putting as you make your chipping stroke. See the line in your mind's eye, especially the spot where you want the ball to land. Make a putting stroke with just enough force to land the ball on that spot.

Stroke with your arms as when putting, move them freely from the shoulder joints. Do not be concerned if your body and legs turn as you stroke. Do not consciously inhibit such movement—let it happen. Actually, on most chip shots you will need some body turn, so your arms can swing freely without bumping into your sides.

When to chip. Once you become fairly proficient with the firm-wristed chipping stroke, it should always be your first choice on close-in shots around the green. The pitching stroke, which I shall describe in the next section, should be used only when chipping is not possible.

When would that be? Well, there is really only one limitation to chipping: distance. The firm-wristed stroke with the putting grip will only make the ball go so far with a given club. When you are beyond that range, you will need to use your normal, full-swing grip, which allows the wrists to cock and uncock. This gives you the extra distance you need.

I can make the ball fly as far as 40 to 50 yards with my chipping stroke. However, your maximum distance will probably be considerably less. If you are a person whose best drives go less than, say, 150 yards, you may find that you cannot chip the ball through the air more than, say, 10 yards, if that.

A little bit of experimenting on the practice range, around the practice green or even in your own yard at home will quickly show you what your maximum chipping distance is.

Once you find your chipping range, and once you develop your chipping technique, apply it on all shots that are within that range. The lie of your ball and the situation at hand—the overall distance to the green and, thereafter, to the flagstick—will largely determine which club you should choose.

Chipping whenever you can gives you the advantages of the firm-wristed stroke: consistent solid contact from even severe lies; a club-head path that stays on line longer than when you stand farther from the ball; a greater potential for squaring the clubface to your line at contact, and, finally, a shot that flies with minimal spin and walks freely forward after landing. As you become more and more proficient with the firm-wristed chipping stroke, still other advantages will become apparent.

For instance, you may find, as I have, that the chipping stroke works better than the pitching stroke even on those short shots where you must make the ball settle quickly upon landing. Imagine that your ball is off to one side of a green. The flagstick is set toward that side, thus leaving you with relatively little landing area. Let's also assume that there is a bunker between your ball and the green.

Given this situation in the past, you may have chosen to play a high pitch shot with the wedge, applying as much backspin as you could to the ball. In doing so, however, you may have found that you often mis-hit the ball and left it short in the sand. Or you may have connected solidly, only to find that the ball came off the clubface too hot and flew too far.

With a certain amount of skill and practice, you can learn to play this shot with the firm-wristed chipping stroke, again using a pitching wedge or a sand wedge for maximum height. With only your arms moving the club—no wrists—the ball will fly slowly through the air. It will plop down gently on the green and settle quickly upon landing, not so much because of backspin, rather because of its high trajectory and generally "soft" flight to the green.

I mention this example to point out that though the chip shot is basically a shot with minimum air length and maximum ground length, it can also be a shot with maximum air length and minimum ground length if you use a highly lofted club.

Again, the only limitation to chipping is length. When you are beyond your chip-shot range, you will need to apply the pitching technique explained in the next section.

SECTION 4: PITCHING

The pitch shot forces us to give up some of those wonderful advantages that help make the chip shot so relatively reliable. We sacrifice these advantages to gain the benefits the pitch shot provides.

It provides more clubhead speed and distance, allowing our ball to reach the target when played from out beyond our chip-shot range. This extra speed also adds height and more backspin, allowing the ball to land on the more predictable surface of the green, yet still settle quickly and stop before running far past the hole.

In short, the pitch shot features *maximum air length* and a happy blend of height and spin for *minimum ground length,* unlike the relatively spin-free, forward-bounding chip shot that incorporates minimum air length and maximum ground length.

Solid Contact: Your First Priority

Pitching is probably the most artistic part of golf. The less-than-full shot from out beyond chipping range puts the priority on subtle skill and discrimination—finesse.

Before I tell you actually how to hold the club, set up to the ball and swing, I think you should understand some of the things you must do, might do and cannot do on these pitching shots.

The first priority on any normal golf shot is reasonably solid contact. Only with such contact can you hope to make the ball go pretty much the distance, direction and height you anticipate.

I mention this fairly obvious priority here, because on pitch shots we do become more vulnerable to misconnection between club and ball. The most common forms of this occur when the clubhead reaches the bottom of its downward-upward arc *before* it arrives at the ball. Apart from shanking (contact made on the hosel, or neck, of the club), this belated contact causes the most disastrous shot results. The clubhead may stub in the turf behind the ball and leave it far short of target, or it may move upward into the ball's backside and blade it low and far across the green.

On the other hand, when the clubhead reaches the bottom of its arc *after* arriving at the ball, when the contact occurs as the clubhead is still moving downward, the results can range from less disastrous to ideal.

Ideal contact occurs when the clubhead reaches the bottom of its arc just a fraction of an inch *in front* of the ball's position, after having met the ball while still moving slightly downward.

Such contact is ideal for most pitch shots because it creates a happy combination of height and backspin. The fact that the clubhead is moving a bit downward at contact creates more backspin than if it were moving level with the ground or upward. This additional backspin creates more friction between the ball and the green upon landing. Thus, it grabs, settles and stops sooner on the putting surface. The added backspin also helps the ball resist gravity to some extent so that in many instances it flies on a higher trajectory, which also makes it stop sooner.

It is true that a downward moving clubhead carries less effective loft than does a level or upward moving clubhead. This reduces height. However, when it comes to reducing ground length, if the clubhead is moving only *slightly* downward at contact, the loss of loft can be more than offset by the addition of spin. Hence, again, the *slightly* downward moving clubhead creates the ideal blend of height and spin.

Now, it is also true that contact will be less than solid if the clubhead reaches the bottom of its arc *too far* in front of the ball's position. However, in most cases, the shot's results will still be less disastrous than if the bottom of the swing occurs behind the ball. The shot may fly lower than you prefer, but it will usually still carry a high degree of backspin.

The point I'm making here is that on normal pitch shots, your chances of fairly solid contact are better on a shot that is slightly *pinched* with the slightly downward moving clubhead than on a shot that is *lobbed* with a level moving clubhead. Also, you will be more likely to achieve the happy combination of height and spin that we need to satisfy the goal of the pitch shot, that being minimum ground length *(see Illustration 24)*.

Surely, by pinching your pitch shots slightly, you will be more likely to eliminate the disaster of making contact with the clubhead moving upward.

The lob pitch has its place, to be sure, especially on shorter pitch shots where the necessarily lesser degree of clubhead speed decreases the amount of backspin that you can apply to the ball. This lesser amount of spin, however, is more than offset by the increased effective loft that results from lobbing the shot. Thus, once again, you enjoy the happy combination of height and spin that you need to minimize the shot's ground length.

Still, the lob shot is riskier than the pinch in that the level-moving clubhead borders on becoming a disastrous, upward-moving club-head. And even the slightly pinched shot is risky from bad lies where grass, turf and the like intervene close in behind the ball. These lies demand a steeper angle of approach, a shot that is severely pinched, for the clubhead to clear the problem area safely and satisfy our first priority of fairly solid contact.

Obviously, the more severely you pinch a shot, the lower the ball will fly because of the club's greatly reduced degree of effective loft. You can offset this loss of height to some extent by making sure that you use your most-lofted club for the shot—the sand wedge, if you happen to have one.

You can also make the ball fly higher on any pitch shot, whether it be lobbed, slightly pinched or severely pinched, by playing a cut shot.

The cut shot, you will recall, features an open clubface at contact. It faces to the right of the direction in which it is moving. If the path of the club is directed to, say, six degrees left of target and the face is aligned

TYPE OF SHOT	SHORT PITCHES		LONG PITCHES	
	SAFETY	STOPPING	SAFETY	STOPPING
LOB WITH CUT	○	○○○○		
LOB	○	○○○○	○	○○○○○
SLIGHT PINCH WITH CUT	○○	○○○○	○○	○○○○○
SLIGHT PINCH	○○	○○○	○○	○○○○○
SEVERE PINCH WITH CUT	○○○	○○○	○○○	○○○○○
SEVERE PINCH	○○○	○○○	○○○	○○○○

24. Safety vs. stopping action on pitch shots

This chart shows six varieties of pitch shots and rates each according to "safety," which is your chance of making solid contact, and "stopping," which represents the tendency of the ball to settle and stop on landing. Again, it is the happy combination of height and degree of backspin that determines the stopping action. The number of balls shown represents the relative degree of safety and stopping action. For instance, the first shot, "Lob With Cut," offers a minimal opportunity for solid contact (one ball shown) but a high degree of stopping action (four balls shown) if solid contact is achieved. No balls are shown for this shot under "Long Pitches," because it is all but impossible to achieve a great deal of length with a given club when the shot is lobbed and cut as well.

only two degrees left of target, then the face is open by four degrees—six degrees less two degrees. You then would have cut the shot by four degrees. The cut adds height to the shot because the more the clubface is open to the right of its path, the greater its effective loft becomes. The more the clubface is closed—facing to the left of its path—the more the effective loft is decreased.

In most cases, cutting a shot also adds additional backspin to the ball. Why? Because the club carries more effective loft on the cut shot and makes contact a bit lower on the ball's backside.

This means that if all other factors are the same, a shot that is cut with an open-faced pitching wedge will backspin more than a shot that is struck with the clubface square, facing in the same direction that the club is moving. A pitching-wedge shot that is struck with the face square will apply more spin than a pitching-wedge shot struck with the clubface closed. The closed face further decreases the effective loft and makes contact occur still higher on the ball.

Finally, a shot that is cut with the face opened to the right of the path will slice *less* to the right than a shot made with a closed clubface will hook to the left. Why? Because the extra backspin applied with the open face has a better chance of negating any slice spin to the right. The closed face applies less backspin to override the hooking effect of the closed face.

Actually, a long pitch shot that is cut with the face opened, say, five degrees to the right, will probably curve only a few inches to the right in flight. Yet, a pitch shot of the same length that is struck with the face closed by five degrees might well curve several feet in flight.

Naturally, upon landing, the cut shot will tend to spin and roll to the right, the hooked shot to the left. However, the hooked shot, lacking in degree of backspin, will not stop as quickly. Its extra ground length will give it more opportunity to bounce and roll farther left than the quick-stopping cut shot can bounce and roll to the right.

To sum up the factors that apply to your pitching game:

—Your first priority is solid contact. The worse the ball's lie, the more you will need to pinch the shot with a downward moving clubhead.

—Pinching the shot tends to decrease height and increase backspin. When you need both maximum height and maximum backspin to make the shot land on the green and stop quickly, choose your most-lofted club, pinch the shot as much as needed for solid contact, but cut the shot as well with the clubface opened to its path. The path should be to the left of target with the face aligned *less to the left,* allowing for some slight curving, bouncing and rolling to the right. (With some experimenting, you will find the maximum amount that you can cut a pitch shot, the amount your clubface can be open to its path without the blow becoming so glancing that the ball merely flops off to the right, far short of the green.)

—When you can hold the green with less than maximum height, pinch the shot as required by the lie, but do not cut the shot. Swing the clubhead into the ball so it moves on line and faces square to that path.

—Do not play normal pitch shots with the clubface closed to the left of its path. In doing so, you will greatly reduce height and backspin, thus increasing the shot's ground length. (While closed-face contact is verboten on normal pitch shots, where the goal is minimum ground length, it is desirable on the so-called "pitch-and-run" shot, which I will explain in the next chapter.)

Pitching Technique

The most significant difference between the chipping and pitching techniques is in the way you hold the club. The grip I suggest for both putting and chipping finds each palm facing midway between directly upward and inward toward the other. The grip I advocate for pitching is the orthodox, full-swing grip.

The main reason for the difference is that when chipping we seek to *disallow* wrist action; when pitching we are forced to *allow*—though not consciously create—some wrist play.

You would find that whenever you assumed the putting grip—by turning your palms more upward—both the top end of the clubshaft and your hands would want to move both upward and outward from your body. As they did, you would feel an increase of tension in your wrists and arms. It is this added tension that helps disallow wrist action when you putt and chip with this grip.

By returning to your full-swing grip, however, you would find that your hands and club wanted to move downward and inward toward your body. You would feel the tension in your wrists and arms disappear. It is this lack of tension that helps allow the wrists to hinge and unhinge when you swing with your normal grip.

Just how should you hold the club on pitch shots? I'll start by using the word "never," one I seldom use in regard to golf, but one I feel is warranted in this case:

On any normal pitch shot, never hold the club with your right palm faced open to the direction you have aimed the clubface. To explain:

You can grip the club with the right palm faced in three general positions. If it faces to the *right* of the direction that the club is aimed, it is facing *open*. If this palm faces in the *same* direction as the club is aimed, it is facing *square*. If it faces to the *left* of the club's aim it is facing *closed* (see Illustration 25).

The problem with an *open* palm at address is that it promotes striking the ball with the clubface itself *closed* to the left. The ball flies too low and carries too little backspin for it to stop quickly upon landing, which is the main reason for pitching the shot in the first place.

Why does facing the right palm to the right at address increase the

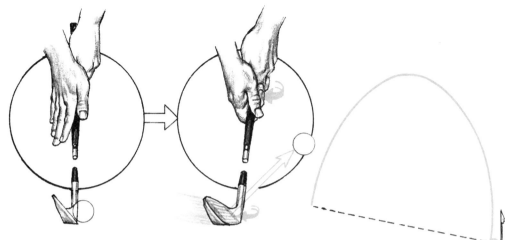

RIGHT HAND CLOSED—YES

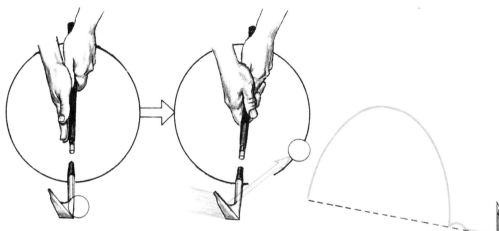

RIGHT HAND PARALLEL—YES

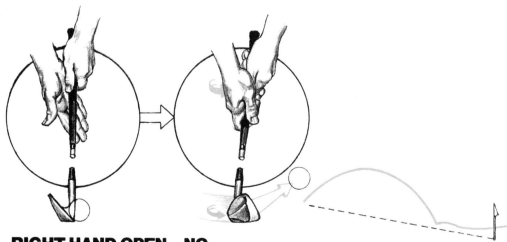

RIGHT HAND OPEN—NO

25. Pitch shot grips

a. Setting the right hand on the club in a "closed" position, with the palm facing to the left of where the club is aimed, is ideal for cutting pitch shots with the face opened to the right of its path at contact. The face becomes opened because this grip makes the hands face less to the left at contact than they did at address.

b. Facing the right palm in the same direction as the club is aimed is best for playing pitch shots that are either lobbed or pinched but not cut with an open clubface. Since this hand positioning is relatively simple to duplicate at contact, the club is likely to return to the same square-to-target facing it was in at address.

c. Setting the right hand in an "open" position, facing to the right of where the club is aimed, is not recommended for normal pitch shots. The hand tends to return to a square facing at contact, thus forcing the clubface to be closed to the left. The closed face delofts the club so that the shot flies too low, to the left, and runs too far upon landing.

risk of closing the clubface to the left at contact? Because, if you swing the club freely, naturally and correctly, this palm will instinctively tend to square itself at contact, just as it would if you clapped your hands together, or spanked a youngster's bottom.

Because of the right hand's natural tendency to swing toward a square facing at contact, we can derive the following relationships, provided, of course, you do make a free and natural swing:

—Gripping with the right palm faced *open*, to the right of where the club is aimed, encourages the clubface to be *closed*, facing to the left of its path, at contact. The normal results: low trajectory, less backspin, more ground length, considerable curve, bounce and roll to the left.

—Gripping with the right palm faced *square*, in the same direction that the club is aimed, encourages the clubface to be square to its path at contact. The normal results: normal height, normal backspin, a straight shot in the direction that the club is moving at contact.

—Gripping with the right palm faced *closed*, to the left of where the club is aimed, encourages the clubface to be *open*, facing to the right of its path, at contact. The normal results: more height, more backspin, less ground length, a slight curve and/or bounce and roll to the right.

If you study in *Illustration 25* the relationships between the positioning of the right hand at address and the character of the shots that are likely to result, it should become evident that:

—A slightly closed right-hand position is best for playing a cut pitch shot, wherein the clubface should be slightly open to its path at contact.

—A square right-hand position is best for playing a straight pitch shot and the so-called "pitch-and-run" shot, as we shall see.

These same general relationships apply to all golf shots on which you use a full-swing grip. On drives, for instance, the more your right hand is open to the right at address, the more your tendency will be to hook the ball low to the left. The more this hand is closed to the left at address, the more you will tend to slice your drives to the right.

On full shots, however, with the longer-shafted clubs, most golfers tend to slice, not hook. For these players, a slightly open hand position at address is advisable in order to eliminate open-faced contact.

The way you position your *left* hand on the club on pitch shots similarly affects the shot's results. It will simplify matters considerably if you set your left hand in the same position on all pitch shots. If you are a strong person, you might be able to control the club with the back of this hand facing in the same direction as you intend to aim the club. A weaker person, especially a woman, will need to face the back of the hand a bit more to the right to maintain sufficient control.

Grip *pressure* is also an important factor in pitching. The main thing that it affects in your swing is the amount that your wrists and arms can contribute. It affects the extent that they can help in (1) making the clubhead swing faster and (2) making it turn from right to left during the forward swing.

The tighter your grip is, the less your wrists and arms can contribute because of the tension created. A tight grip tends to inhibit clubhead speed and your chances of squaring the clubface to the line by contact; it tends to produce shorter shots and open-faced contact.

Conversely, a light grip reduces wrist and arm tension, so long as it remains light all the way through contact. It allows you to make a longer swing, create more clubhead speed (distance) and to contact the ball with a square or, perhaps, closed clubface.

We do need a certain degree of firmness in the left-hand grip on all shots because this is the hand that should, in large part, control the club. However, the right hand's pressure can vary with the length of the shot.

On drives and other distance shots, a light right-hand grip is ideal for creating maximum clubhead speed (more length) and minimizing any tendency toward slicing due to open-faced contact.

A fairly light right-hand grip is fine for most golfers on the longer pitch shots where a fair amount of distance is needed from the highly lofted clubs. On shorter pitch shots, however, I advocate a firm grip in both hands. These shots require less air length and, therefore, less clubhead speed. The fact that you have already departed from your wrist-inhibiting, putting-chipping grip will, in itself, allow enough wrist and arm freedom to create sufficient speed. Additional wrist play complicates making solid contact and increases your chances of closing the clubface too soon.

The firm grip is actually advantageous on these shorter pitch shots. Because of their close-in nature, we cannot rely too much on clubhead speed for creating the height and backspin we need to make the ball stop quickly. It would fly too far as well.

The firm grip, however, tends to create open-faced contact, which increases the club's effective loft. This makes the ball fly higher and backspin more than it otherwise might, given such a relatively slow-moving clubhead. In short, the firm grip allows you to swing more aggressively on close-in pitch shots. This makes the ball fly high with considerable backspin, yet not so far that it lands well past the flagstick.

My final point about gripping has to do with how far down the shaft you should hold the club. The farther down on the shaft you grip, the more you are shortening the weapon you are swinging. Since the shorter implement creates less distance, by gripping down on the club you can swing more aggressively on part shots without the ball flying too far. You can be more positive in your stroking action.

Gripping down on the club also tends to decrease wrist play. By shortening the *effective* length of the club, you also decrease the *effective* weight of the club's head. It becomes easier for *you* to control the club, less likely that *it* will control you, by forcing your wrists to cock and uncock unduly in reaction to its weight.

26. Grip down, bend forward

While the plane of the golf swing should be neither horizontal (top illustration) nor vertical (middle illustration), it should tend more toward the vertical, especially on pitch shots. The more upright plane is more likely to create the height and backspin needed to make the shot settle quickly upon landing. Gripping well down on the clubshaft allows you to bend well forward from the hips at address, thus presetting yourself to swing on a relatively upright plane.

Finally, gripping down on the clubshaft allows you—indeed forces you—to stand closer to the ball. This brings you closer to your work—for better control of contact. It also helps make your clubhead swing and face on line for a longer duration through the contact area, much like it does when you set your eyes directly over the line when putting.

For all of these reasons, I advocate that on pitch shots you not hold the club any farther up the shaft than is necessary to make the shot fly the required distance. Hold it down near the bottom of the "leather" on close-in pitches and progressively higher as the need for creating a longer stroke increases.

There is still another advantage to gripping down on the shaft on pitch shots. By shortening the effective length of the club, you can bend a bit more forward than normal at address without digging the club into the ground under the ball during your swing. This extra degree of forward-bending allows you to swing the club naturally on a more upright plane, which is ideal for pitch shots in general, but especially so on the pitch shots you wish to cut.

On every golf shot, we must swing the club on a plane that is somewhere between perfectly upright (vertical) and perfectly flat (horizontal). It will help you understand this concept if you imagine that you have a large propeller strapped across your shoulders. As you swing, this propeller will turn around your suspension point, that bump at the nape of your neck.

If you were to swing while standing upright, with your spinal column vertical, this propeller would turn like the prop on a helicopter—on a perfectly flat plane.

The more you bent your spinal column forward, the more this propeller would turn on a more upright plane, more like the turning of an airplane's prop (see Illustration 26).

On pitch shots, we want the swing to be more akin to the airplane propeller than the helicopter propeller. We want to bend well forward, which the shorter grip on the club allows us to do.

The relatively upright swing is best on pitch shots for several reasons, but mainly because it is more likely to make the ball fly higher

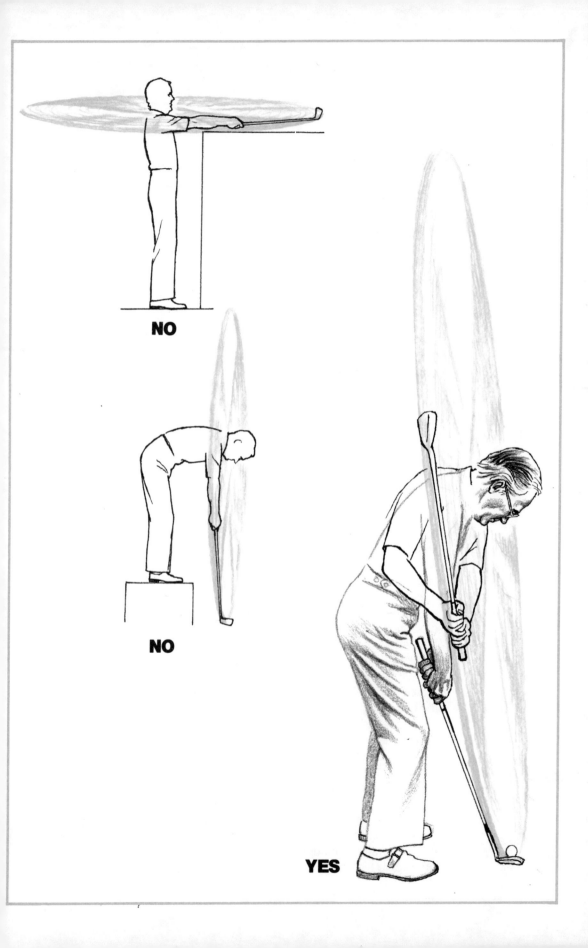

NO

NO

YES

with more backspin, the two ingredients you need to make it stop quickly upon landing. The ball flies higher with more backspin because the upright swing is:

1. A steeper swing. The clubhead moves more dramatically upward and then downward if your swing is more like the turning of an airplane's propeller than that of the helicopter. Its steeply downward angle of approach is ideal for pinching the ball and applying backspin. Also, since the force of the blow is more downward and less forward, you can swing more firmly, more positively, without the shot flying too far.

The flatter swing makes this angle of approach too shallow, too close to being level, which increases the risk that the clubhead will either stub in the ground behind the ball or blade the ball with the club's leading edge already moving upward.

2. A more on-line swing. When the swing plane is more akin to that of an airplane propeller, the clubhead moves less *to* the inside of the line during the backswing and can move less *from* the inside during its return to the ball. Instead, it swings up and down on a path that is more closely allied with the target line itself.

This greater degree of on-line movement is important because of the way our wrists and arms react to the path of the swing.

The flatter the swing is—the more we swing around ourselves—the easier it becomes for the arms and wrists to turn the clubface naturally counterclockwise, from opened to closed, right to left, during the forward swing. This increases the risk of making closed-faced contact, which hooks the ball to the left on a lower trajectory with less backspin. If you have played Ping-Pong, this stroke is more like the type you would make on a forehand smash.

The more upright, on-line swing impedes this leftward, counter-clockwise turning of the arms and wrists during the forward stroke. In fact, an extremely upright swing plane may cause them to turn clockwise slightly. This opens the clubface slightly and further increases the shot's height and the ball's spin. This stroking action is more like the Ping-Pong player's cut shot, in which the ball barely clears the net and then pulls up and spins to the right.

As far as actual technique is concerned, the point to remember here is that you are more likely to swing on the ideal, relatively upright plane if you bend a bit more forward at address. The more upright your spinal column is—the taller you stand—the greater your tendency will be to swing the club around yourself on a less desirable, relatively flat plane.

In this regard, I've always felt that Ralph Guldahl, winner of the U.S. Open in 1937 and 1938, excelled on pitch shots largely because he was extremely stoop-shouldered. His normal posture was perfect for producing the upright swing.

The only danger in bending well forward on these shots is that doing so might make you dig the clubhead into the ground under the ball. Or, in reaction to such digging, you might tend to lift yourself during your downswing and top the shot.

To avoid these problems, set your hands far enough down on the club's grip so that you can extend your arms at address, just as they will be extended at contact.

Also, be sure to sole the club only lightly on the grass at address, just as I have suggested for putting and chipping. Feel that the weight of the club is in your hands, not on the ground. In short, address the ball itself, not the ground behind it.

Checklist. In reviewing my pitching instruction, I will mention both the basics and the modifications that are required for certain specific types of pitch shots.

Grip: Use your full-swing grip, but make sure that your right palm faces either in the *same* direction you intend to aim the clubface (palm square) or slightly to the left of that direction (palm closed). The more you want to cut the shot with an open clubface at contact, the more your right palm should face to the left at address.

Apply enough left-hand grip pressure on all pitch shots to control the club. Apply a similarly firm pressure with the right hand on short pitch shots—where relatively little wrist action and swing length is needed to create distance—and on cut shots, to inhibit the wrists and arms from closing the clubface.

Lighten your right-hand pressure on the longer shots where you must make a longer swing with increased wrist freedom to create sufficient distance.

Grip as far down on the leather as you can within the limits of creating sufficient distance. The shorter the shot, the farther down the shaft you can, and should, set your hands.

Address: Bend well forward from the hips on all pitch shots to create a relatively upright swing plane.

Sole the clubhead lightly on the grass. Feel the weight of the club in your hands, not on the ground.

Stand no farther away from the line than you must to (1) sole the club, (2) extend your left arm *downward* and (3) allow room for the arms to swing freely. Do not stand so far away that you must reach outward with your arms. This reaching outward will tend to flatten your swing plane.

Aim the clubface down your target line on shots that you do not wish to cut. Aim it very slightly to the left of target on short shots that you wish to cut, and farther left on longer cut shots.

On shots you do not wish to cut, align your feet and body parallel with the direction you aimed the clubface. On cut shots, align a bit more to the left of where you've aimed the club.

Play the ball just inside your left heel on shots you wish to lob, and distribute your weight evenly between the two feet. (Remember, lob shots imply a level-moving clubhead at contact and require that the ball be setting up on the grass.)

On short shots that you wish to pinch *slightly*, set more weight onto your left foot—lean your suspension point to the left. On short shots you wish to pinch more severely, lean left and play the ball farther back to the right in your stance as well, according to the severity of the pinch required.

On longer pitch shots you want to pinch, you should not lean to the left as on short pinch shots, rather play the ball back to the right in your stance, again according to the degree you wish the clubhead to be moving downward at contact.

Swing: The goal on most pitch shots is to make the ball "float" through the air so that it will settle gently on the green. Therefore, it is best to reduce as much as possible the rapid acceleration that the quick-moving hands and wrists tend to create. Instead, it is best to increase the contribution made by the slower-moving muscles of the legs and hips. Feel that you are creating distance more with your lower body and less with your hands and arms. You will probably need to stress this lower-body influence more on your shorter pitch shots, where it is less likely to occur naturally, than on longer pitch shots where you may already be using your legs and hips sufficiently.

Unless your swing is normally a bit upright, you should consciously try to make it more upright on pitch shots, more akin to the plane on which an airplane propeller turns.

Swing on this upright plane, but also on a path that is allied to your feet and body alignment at address. Thus, on non-cut pitch shots you should swing upright on a path that is identical to the direction you aimed the clubface. On cut shots, you should swing the clubhead into the ball on a path that is directed slightly to the left of where you aimed the club.

Pitch-and-run shot. This is a pitch shot in one sense but not in another.

It is a pitch shot in that you use it when you are within part-swing distance of the green, but out beyond your chip-shot range. Its length requires you to use your normal full-swing grip, rather than your wrist-inhibiting, putting-chipping grip.

It is *not* a pitch shot, however, in the sense that the goal is minimum ground length. We do not want the ball to fly high with lots of backspin so that it stops quickly upon landing; rather, we want the ball to bounce and roll freely forward.

When might this be? The most common occasion is when you must land the ball short of the putting surface when you do not have sufficient green area for a normal pitch, or even a cut-pitch, to land on the surface yet stop in time. The pitch-and-run shot works well in this situation, because it "walks through" the longer grass surrounding the green.

It also works well when you must play short of the green with a low-flying shot that must go under, say, a tree limb.

At times the pitch-and-run can also be used when you actually intend to land the ball on the green. Suppose the green is two-level and the flagstick is set on the higher back level. You decide you cannot pitch to that upper level and still make the ball stop on the green. So you pitch and run the shot, landing the ball on the lower level with enough forward momentum for it to bounce and roll up to the second tier.

In regard to this kind of situation, let me underline once again that you should play your firm-wristed chip shot whenever you are within range of reaching the target. Only when beyond that range would you play the pitch-and-run shot. And even then you would not play a pitch-and-run shot to land short of the green, if you could land on the green and stop the ball in time with a standard pitch shot.

To make the pitch shot run, you will need to contact the ball with the clubface closed to its path, facing a bit to the left of where the clubhead is moving.

In this case, you should grip the club with your right palm facing in the same direction as you aim the club. Also, hold the club lightly in this hand all the way through contact with the ball to avoid any grabbing that might inhibit the turning of the clubface from right to left.

Aim the club slightly to the right of where you want the shot to start out, but align yourself even more to the right. During the forward stroke, try to turn the club counterclockwise, from right to left, with your arms, so that the toe of the club will pass the heel at contact with the ball. (The technique for playing the pitch-and-run shot is the same you might well use on full shots when your goal is to hook the ball intentionally.)

SECTION 5:
YOUR PART-SHOT
GAME PLAN

Any shotmaking situation you face on the golf course has more than one solution. This is especially true in part-shot situations around the green in which you might literally have dozens of different options on a single shot. Often you will have the choice of playing the shot with three or four or more different clubs. You might have the options of lobbing the shot, or pinching it slightly or severely, with any one of those clubs. You could cut the shot or not cut it. You might have the choice between playing a chip shot or a pitch shot, between landing the ball short of the green or on the green. And you might have various landing spots on the green from which to choose.

For you to select the option that gives you the best chance for success with the least amount of risk, you should have a game plan—a system or procedure for deciding which shot to play.

I will give you such a system with some guidelines you should consider before you play any part shot to a green.

If you have never used a system before, if you have played all of these shots more or less the same way with the same club, you will need to digest my suggestions. In time, through continued application, it will become second nature for you to choose the best option in a given situation with very little conscious thought.

Before I give you my guidelines, however, I would like to make one important point: While there is a best way to handle any given part-shot situation, you should not play the shot that way if you lack the skill to do so. As much as I abhor seeing a golfer putt the ball from several feet off the green to a distant flagstick, I would never blame that player for putting instead of chipping if he happened to be a poor chipper.

Step 1—Check the lie. In the game plan I recommend, the way the ball sets is the first thing you should study. Unfortunately, it is the one consideration most golfers overlook. Yet any chance of making a successful shot depends above all on making fairly solid contact with the ball. And it is the lie of the ball that determines what you must do to make such contact.

As a general rule, the worse the ball's lie, the more severely will you need to pinch the shot to make solid contact. Most bad lies require pinching so the club can move into the ball on a descending angle of approach and avoid snagging in the grass or the ground behind it.

In practical terms, this means that in most cases the worse the lie is, the farther to the target side of the ball you will need to preset your suspension point to achieve enough pinch to contact the ball first and then the turf, rather than the turf and then the ball.

The more aware you become of various types of lies and how the ball reacts from each type, the better you will become at prejudging the amount of pinch you will need on a given shot. Here are some common types of lies, presented more or less in their order of difficulty.

Ball setting well atop a substantial cushion of grass. This is the ideal lie. It allows contacting the underside of the ball, even if you play a lob shot with a level angle of approach.

Ball setting atop tightly cropped grass, such as on the fringe area of the green. Here, because there is less grass under the ball, you will probably need a slight degree of pinch for the club to catch the ball's underside without digging into the ground as it does or slightly before it does. Preset your suspension a bit to the left by leaning onto your left foot.

Ball setting down in fairway grass but with some cushion of grass beneath it. Here again you will need some pinch to minimize the amount of grass that the club must pass through before it reaches the ball. The deeper it sets in the grass, the more you will need to lean left at address and, in deep fairway grass and rough, also play the ball back in your stance.

Ball setting on bare, but level, ground. Since there is no cushion under the ball, you will need even more pinch as a safety margin against your club's catching in the ground behind it. Play the ball back a bit in your stance and lean left.

Ball setting in a depression, such as a divot mark, or on bare ground with a bump of ground or a sprig of coarse grass just behind it, or in deep or thick rough. These are the lies that require a severe degree of pinch. Play the ball well back in your stance, perhaps even opposite your right foot, and lean left.

If there is a general theme to be found within this discussion of lies, it would be that the situation demands more severe action as the amount of grass under the ball lessens and the height of grass or the ground immediately behind it increases.

Step 2—Visualize your shot. Once you have checked the lie and decided what you must do to make solid contact with the ball, your next step should be to determine what you want the ball to do to finish in or near the hole.

This step requires you to put your imagination to work. You will need to visualize the different shots that the situation allows you to play and then decide on the one shot you think is most likely to succeed.

To make this decision, your first question should be, "Can I land the ball on the green and still make it stop without going too far past my target?" Landing the ball on the smoother putting surface is almost always preferable to landing it short of the green, where it can easily snag in the longer grass and/or bounce off line from the rougher landing surface.

In deciding whether or not you can land the ball on the green and still stop it in time, you will need to consider, of course, the lie of the ball. If it is a bad lie that requires a severe degree of pinch to make solid contact, your shot will tend to fly quite low and run quite far. Thus, in some cases, the lie itself will all but disallow landing the ball on the green, even if you were to cut the shot with your most-lofted club.

Assuming you can land the ball on the green, your next question should be, "Where on the green should I make it land?"

Here you may have a choice between (a) playing a relatively low-flying shot that carries a relatively short distance, lands just a few feet onto the green, then bounces and rolls the rest of the way, or (b) playing a relatively high shot that carries a relatively long distance, well onto the green, and then settles quickly to a halt in a relatively short distance.

In other words, your choice could be either a shot that has (a) minimum air length and maximum ground length or (b) maximum air length and minimum ground length. You could also compromise to some degree between these two extremes.

Given these two choices, I feel the odds for success greatly favor the low-flying shot—minimum air length, maximum ground length—the shot that lands no farther forward onto the green than is necessary to avoid any risk of it landing short of the putting surface altogether (*see Illustration 27*).

There are several reasons why the low, running chip shot is better than the high-flying, soft-settling pitch shot:

—The lower-flying shot allows you to choose a less-lofted club. From normal lies it is easier to contact the ball solidly with this less-lofted club. (To appreciate this fact, consider what your chances would be of striking putts solidly if you were forced to putt with your highly lofted pitching wedge.)

—To play the low-flying, running shot with a less-lofted club, your

27. Visualize your options

Training yourself to visualize the various short approach shots you might play in a given situation is a vital aspect of short-game strategy. Here we see two such options, both of which are worthwhile in that the ball lands on the green. The shot with minimum air length and maximum ground length is preferable, because: (a) it allows the

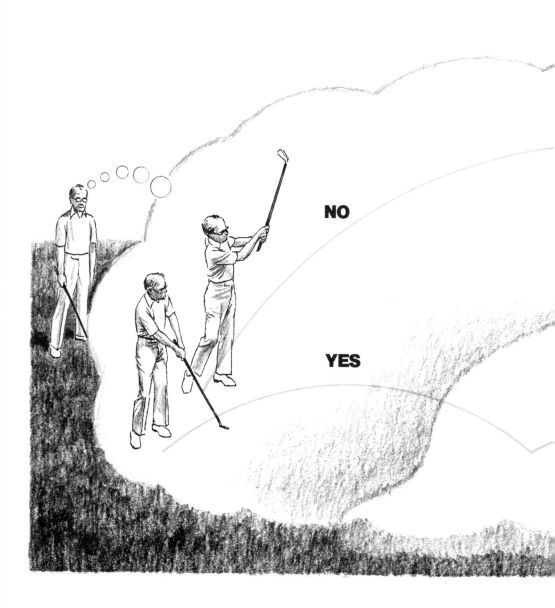

NO

YES

use of a lesser-lofted club, which is more likely to create solid contact than a highly lofted club; (b) it allows the player to make a shorter, less-complex swing; (c) the player is more likely to land the ball on his intended landing spot because it is closer to him; (d) the lower flying ball is more likely to bounce forward than sideways, and (e) the lower shot is less likely to be affected by any wind.

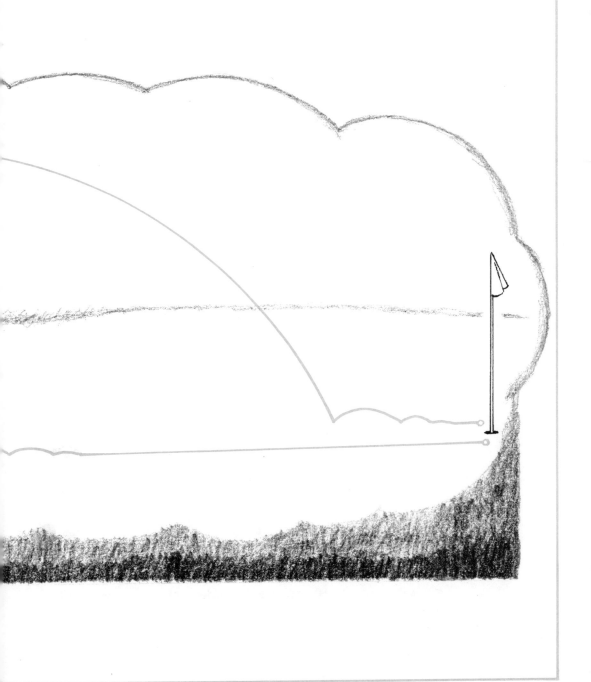

swing does not need to be nearly as long or as complex as the swing needed to make the ball carry higher and farther with a more-lofted club.

—It is easier to land the ball on or near a given spot on the green if that spot is relatively close to where you are playing the shot from.

—The lower-flying shot falls to the green on a shallower, more-forward angle of descent than does the highly lofted shot, as shown in *Illustration 27*. It is less likely to indent itself into the putting surface upon landing. The less indentation the ball makes, the more predictable its forward thrust becomes. This makes the bounce and roll on a low-flying shot more predictable, especially if some parts of the green happen to be relatively soft and other parts relatively firm, as is often the case.

—The lower shot is less susceptible to wind influences. Playing it minimizes the need to consider this somewhat unpredictable variable.

For all of these reasons, the shot to play in most instances is the low-flying, running shot that lands on the green on a spot that is as close as possible to the edge but not so close as to risk its landing short.

In deciding whether or not you can play this low, running shot and still stop the ball in time, you will need to visualize the trajectory of the shot. You will need to "see" that trajectory and then decide how far the ball will bounce and roll after landing. There may not be enough surface of the green to allow landing on it and still make the ball stop in time. This would be even more likely if the green were especially fast or it sloped downward to the hole.

I suggest you also consider the terrain of the green, just as you would on a putt. There will be times when, for instance, you face a severe uphill slope on the front part of the green. Your options might be to: (a) play a low-flying, running shot into the slope; (b) play a higher shot with more carry that would land beyond the slope and closer to the hole, or (c) play a low, running shot that lands short of the green itself and runs up the slope to the hole.

So, obviously, choosing the best shot to play in a given situation requires you to be particularly aware of that situation—the lie, the texture of the green, the terrain, the amount of green between you and the hole, and so on.

I once lost the Miami Open to Gene Sarazen—whom I dearly loved to beat and thoroughly hated losing to—simply because I failed to notice an old, dried-up ball mark on the 18th green. I played what I thought was an excellent chip shot just onto the green, but it landed in that mark and all but stopped dead some 30 to 35 feet short of the hole. I two-putted and he took the title by a shot.

Choosing the best shot also means choosing the best shot for *you*. Go with the shot that the odds, as I have described them, favor. But if you lack confidence and skill on that particular shot, you should play a less favorable one you know you can play correctly.

Finally, being a good short-game player requires that you develop the ability to visualize beforehand the various shot options available to you in a given situation. It will take you some time and concentrated effort to actually "see" shots in flight, then landing, bouncing and rolling forward. But you can develop this talent if you try. The ability to visualize and then execute a wide variety of shots from around the greens is the real key to becoming a master of the short game.

Step 3—Choose the right club. By now you have checked the lie and picked the spot where you want the ball to land. You have visualized the particular trajectory your shot will need for it to land on or near that spot and bounce and roll to the flagstick.

Your next step is to choose the club that will produce the shot you have just visualized, keeping in mind that the more you intend to pinch the shot the lower it will fly, and that the more you plan to cut the shot the higher it will fly.

For instance, you have a short shot to the green. Your ball is about 10 feet off the edge of the putting surface. The hole is about 30 feet beyond. The green is fairly level. It is not unusually firm or soft. It was mowed that morning, so it is not unusually slow.

You have decided to land the ball as close as you can to a spot some five feet onto the green, thus giving yourself a five-foot margin of safety against landing short of it in the longer grass. In effect, you have decided to play a shot that I feel the odds favor, a shot with minimum air length and maximum ground length.

You have visualized the flight of a shot that will land on that spot and, thereafter, bounce and roll to the hole, The trajectory you have visualized is that which you might normally expect to get from a club with, say, a 6-iron loft.

However, you have also noted that the ball is setting down a bit in the fairway grass. You've decided that you will need to pinch it to make solid contact.

You know that pinching the shot with the 6-iron, striking the ball with a descending angle of approach, will reduce the club's effective loft. At contact, that loft might be lessened to that of, say, a 4-iron.

Thus, if you were to pinch the shot with the 6-iron, it would fly to your landing spot on the lower trajectory of a 4-iron. The lower trajectory would make it bounce and roll farther than you had intended. Even if the ball were to land on the spot you had chosen, it would still not stop rolling until it was several feet past the hole.

In this situation, you would be wiser to play the same shot but with an 8-iron instead of the 6-iron. Pinching the 8-iron would reduce its effective loft to the built-in loft of the 6-iron. Thus the 8-iron, when pinched, would give you the 6-iron trajectory that you had planned to create (*see Illustration 28*).

In that same situation, but with the ball in an even less desirable lie, one that required a still greater degree of pinch to assure solid contact,

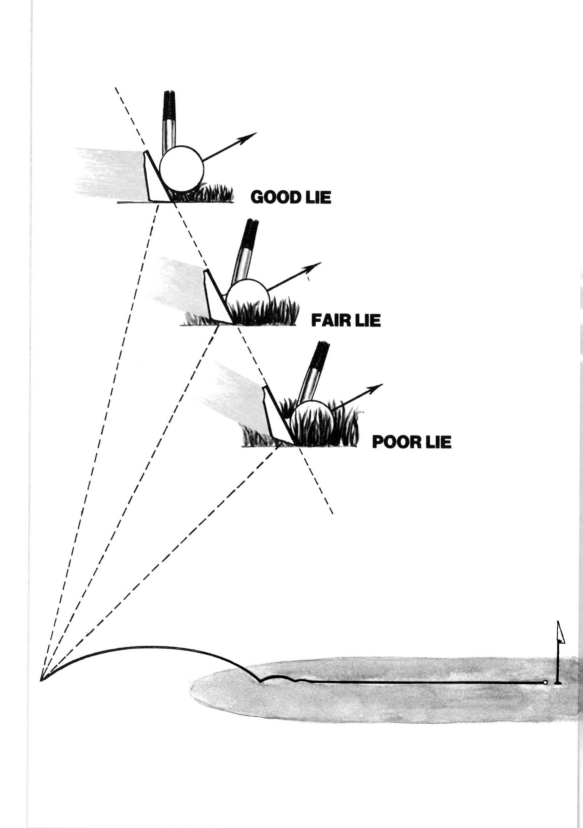

GOOD LIE

FAIR LIE

POOR LIE

28. Choosing the right club

a. The club you should use on any given, short approach shot depends on the trajectory of the shot you have visualized and the lie of the ball in the grass. Here we have a shot that is similar to the preferred option shown in Illustration 27. It would apear to be a shot that should fly on the trajectory most golfers might expect from a 6- or 7-iron. If the lie were good enough to allow solid contact with a level moving clubhead, the golfer could use a 6- or 7-iron to achieve that particular trajectory.

b. If, however, the ball sat down in the grass a bit, the player would need a slightly descending angle of approach to assure solid contact. This angle would take effective loft off the club. Thus he might need to play the shot with an 8- or 9-iron to produce the desired 6- or 7-iron trajectory.

c. A bad lie would require a still steeper angle of approach to make solid contact. The additionally lessened effective loft that would result requires the choice of a 9-iron or a wedge to produce a shot of 6- or 7-iron trajectory.

you would need to choose a club with still more built-in loft. You might need the built-in loft of a pitching wedge to create the effective loft, and thus the trajectory, of the 6-iron.

Now, what would you do if you were the same distance from that same green but with the flagstick, say, only 18 feet from the edge? To make the ball land that same, safe five feet onto the green, you would need to play a shot with a much higher trajectory. Only then could it possibly land on that spot, yet settle and stop quickly enough to finish near the hole instead of far past it. This shot might need to fly on the normal trajectory of, say, a pitching wedge.

Given an excellent lie, you could actually lob the shot with the pitching wedge.

If the lie were slightly less favorable, you could possibly pinch it a bit with your more-lofted sand wedge and achieve the same pitching-wedge trajectory you desire.

If the lie were even worse, you might choose to pinch the shot a bit more severely with the sand wedge, but cut it slightly as well. The extra pinch would normally make the sand wedge fly the ball on a 9-iron trajectory—too low for the shot at hand—but the opened clubface involved in cutting the shot would add enough effective loft to, once again, create the pitching-wedge trajectory.

If, given such a lie, you decided you lacked the skill both to pinch and cut the shot, you would need only to pinch it to assure solid contact. However, you would do so with the realization that the ball would fly lower and run farther. Therefore, you would need to take the chance that you could either land the ball closer to the edge of the green—just a foot or two onto the surface—or you would need to forget about landing it on the green at all. Instead, you would plan the shot to land short of the putting surface.

Again, these are ideal shots to play from around the green; but if they are not part of your current level of skill, you will need to play a less-than-ideal shot you feel you have the ability to create.

Step 4—Rehearse the stroke. Now that you have chosen the club you think will produce the shot you desire from the lie you have, it comes time to program yourself to make the ball land on the spot you have chosen. In effect, you will be giving yourself the feel of the stroke you hope to play.

While I hate to see golfers take two or three practice swings on full shots where the swing will be of more or less maximum length and effort, I do feel that part shots usually require several rehearsal swings. On these shots, the golfer needs to tone down his swing effort to the precise fraction he needs to make the ball fly a specific fraction of its normal, full length.

If you study the pre-swing routines of touring pros, you will find that very few take more than one practice swing on full shots, but almost all make several practice swings before playing a part shot.

Make your practice swings unobtrusively while others are playing their shots or walking to their balls. Make these swings with your suspension point in the same position you intend it to be in on your actual shot. As you make these swings, refer continually to the spot where you intend to make the shot land. Your goal is to find the degree and force of stroke you need to accomplish that goal.

Step 5—Duplicate your rehearsal stroke. Once you can *feel* the stroke you wish to make, set the club behind the ball and get yourself into position according to the type of shot you wish to play, whether it be a lob, pinch, cut-lob or cut-pinch.

At this point, I think you should trust the fact that you have programmed yourself to make a correct stroke. Do not think about how you will stroke the ball. Instead, visualize the shot you wish to play. See the ball flying through the air, landing on the spot you have chosen and bouncing and rolling to the hole.

As you actually swing the club on shots from off the green, you should have nothing on your mind except landing the ball on your chosen spot. On putts, you should make the stroke with an overall visualization of the ball rolling down your intended line and into the hole.

Please study and reflect on the game plan I have suggested on these pages. Developing a similar procedure is as important for your game as actually developing the correct physical technique for playing part shots. You could develop the world's greatest putting, chipping and pitching techniques, yet still remain a relatively mediocre short-game player if you failed to consider all your options around the green and make sensible decisions about them.

SECTION 6:
SAND PLAY

I doubt that any golfer who played in the Charleston Open during the 1930's will ever forget the 11th hole at the Charleston Country Club's Wapoo Links.

It was not a long hole, only 172 yards from the back of the tees, but the green was extremely narrow and tilted slightly to the right. And any tee shot that missed to the left or right finished in deep bunkers that closely guarded each side.

The sand on the left was about 10 feet below the putting surface. The trap on the right was even deeper. Many a player volleyed shot after shot back and forth across the slim green, occasionally rifling one into the bank to break the monotony. Scores on the par-3 hole often ran into double figures.

Few survived. Henry Picard, the resident professional at Charleston, had one solution. He would bunt his tee shot down the fairway so that it finished short of the green, and the sand. Then he'd chip up, putt out for par or bogey and go on about his business.

I had a different ploy. I'd found a way to make my sand shot pop up high enough to clear the walls of those bunkers, yet settle quickly near the flagstick. Thanks largely to this shot, my cumulative score on this particular hole, over the years, was one under par.

My sand technique evolved in part from observing how John Revolta played these shots. Among the golfers of that era, I would rank myself second, along with Sam Snead, out of bunkers. But Revolta led the class by a big margin. His skill from sand simply left me aghast.

Basic Sand Technique

First, you should appreciate that the basic sand shot is really nothing more than a controlled fat shot. The clubhead enters the sand *behind* the ball, so the sand itself cushions the force of the blow. This allows you to make a fairly full and aggressive swing without flying the ball into the next county.

To play these shots by contacting the ball and not using the sand would require a short, dainty stroke. Then, should the clubhead happen to catch any sand at all before reaching the ball, it would lack the velocity to carry the shot from the bunker.

Swinging the club into the sand behind the ball was in vogue even in the 30's. The difference between the Revolta method and that used by most other players was in the angle at which the clubhead moved into the sand. Most swung on a more or less normal arc so the clubhead entered on a slightly downward angle of approach.

Revolta and Runyan, however, chose to swing the club up and down at a much steeper angle. Our swing was more "V" shaped.

This shape of swing allows you to be more precise in making the club enter the sand at a specific point behind the ball. Let's say you wanted to bang someone squarely on the toe with your clubhead. You'd chop downward. If you didn't, you'd be more likely to swing into the side of his shoe, or into the ground beforehand, or over the top of the shoe altogether.

The V-shaped swing also allows you to be more aggressive without the shot flying far. The more downward the clubhead is moving, the more its force is absorbed by the sand. The more forward moving clubhead flies the ball farther, often too far.

Also, when played correctly, the V-shaped swing puts more backspin on the ball. Thus it flies upward higher and stops faster upon landing.

Finally, the clubhead's extremely downward movement all but assures that the club will penetrate the sand and move under the ball. A shallower approach angle sometimes causes the clubhead to bounce off the sand and into the back or top of the ball. Or it misses the sand altogether and merely skulls the ball low and far (see *Illustration 29*).

The golfers who suffered most on the 11th hole at Charleston were those who played sand shots with a clubhead angle of approach that was too shallow. Sometimes they flew the shots low and hard into the bank. Even their best efforts still flew too low and too far to hold the narrow green.

There are times when you need a longer sand shot. Then, as I shall explain later, the shallower angle of approach has its place. For the moment, however, I am talking about what I consider to be the ideal way to play a *normal* greenside bunker shot, when you want the ball to fly high but not too far, and to stop fairly quickly on what is usually a fairly limited landing area.

Here the V-shaped swing is your best ticket. You simply pick the club up abruptly at a sharp angle on your backswing. You return it downward at that same angle on your downswing. The sole of the clubhead begins to bruise the sand an inch or two behind the ball. A bit of sand passes over the clubface as it moves under the ball. This creates a sandpaper effect between the clubface and the ball. It puts a great deal of backspin on the ball, giving the shot both height and additional stopping action.

Before you swing, however, be sure to settle your feet comfortably into the sand for a sure footing. Play the ball an inch or two inside—to the right of—your left foot. Also set a little more weight on your left foot than on your right. This helps you swing the club up and down on a sharper angle.

However, don't let your hands get so far ahead of the clubhead at address that you deloft its face. Your club's shaft should extend upward more or less vertically if you are standing on a level surface, as shown in *Illustration 29*, or at a right angle to the surface if you're on a downslope or an upslope.

Finally, hold the club firmly with both hands. This will restrict your wrist action and increase your precision. It will also eliminate any loosening of the grip when the club encounters the sand. The basic sand-shot swing relies largely on the arms, legs and body, not on the wrists, to create club movement. If you hold the club with the same firmness on both short and long sand shots, the clubhead's lesser or greater velocity will automatically create the lesser or greater degree of wrist action you need for the distance at hand.

The sand club. By now you may have wondered how in the world you could possibly make a V-shaped swing without burying the club deep in the sand behind the ball. All past experience tells us that the more steeply downward we chop or cut into something —a log with an axe, a stick of butter with a knife—the deeper we penetrate.

Well, it all depends on the implement you have in hand. The axe and the butterknife do cut deeply because both are sharp-edged. But what if you turned the axe or the knife to its side, so the sharp edge was not

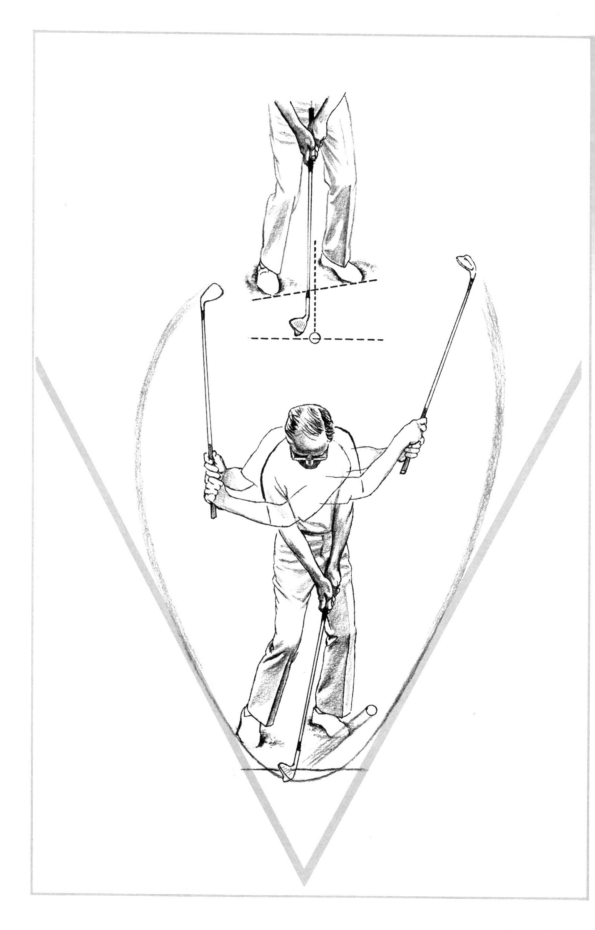

29. The "V"-shaped sand shot

The basic sand shot is more or less "V" shaped. The arms swing the club steeply upward and then downward into the sand behind the ball. The clubhead bruises the sand under the ball and rebounds steeply upward on the follow-through. The steepness of the swing helps assure that the clubhead penetrates under the ball. The ball flies high and soft and settles quickly upon landing. Dig your feet well into the sand beforehand and grip the club firmly to prevent excessive wrist action. Weight should be set more onto the left foot at address to increase backswing steepness, but the clubshaft should be more or less vertical, not tilted forward.

aimed downward? Then you could attack the log or the butter as steeply as you wished, hardly indenting either.

A good sand wedge is uniquely designed to let you make a downward, V-shaped swing without burying the head in the sand. It is built so its sole can merely *bruise* the sand. The club does move downward and forward into the sand a slight amount, but just enough to slide barely under the ball. Then it rebounds upward and forward, completing the second side of the "V."

The sole of a good sand wedge incorporates one or both of two features that allow it to resist deep penetration.

One feature is the sole's width, as measured from its leading edge to its trailing edge. The wider the sole is, the less the club will penetrate, even with a sharply descending blow.

The second feature to resist penetrating too deeply is the sole's "inversion" or "bounce." This is the degree that its trailing edge is *lower* than its leading edge. The greater the inversion—the more the sole slopes upward from back to front—the less it will penetrate. *(Sole inversion is shown clearly in Illustration 30.)*

Here the principle is the same as we saw applied in the old days when basements were excavated with a team of horses pulling a large shovel or scoop. When he wanted to cut downward into the ground, the man guiding the shovel would lift up on the handles. This lowered the shovel's leading edge. When he wanted the shovel to come out of the ground, he would push down on the handles, thus lowering the shovel's trailing edge and raising the leading edge. In effect, he was creating the same inversion of the shovel's bottom that we need on the sole of a good sand wedge.

Other iron clubs in the bag do not have an inverted sole. Since these clubs penetrate so readily, the player will frequently leave the shot in the bunker. The golfer who tries to play sand shots with a 9-iron or a pitching wedge faces a huge and unnecessary problem.

In my opinion, the sole of a good sand wedge should have 10 to 12 degrees of inversion and three-eighths to one-half inch of width. If the inversion is 12 degrees, the width should be three-eighths of an inch. If it's 10 degrees, the width should be one-half inch. If the inversion is only

8 degrees, you'd better have a width of at least five-eighths of an inch, or three-quarters of an inch if the inversion is only 6 degrees. If the club has little or no inversion, if the leading and trailing edges are of equal height, then the sole should be at least one inch to one and a half inches wide.

You will find that the sole on some sand wedges is rounded, convex. The leading and trailing edges are about the same height, but the middle part is lower than either. The Hogan "Sure-Out" has this configuration. I think it is probably the best sand club ever made for Mr. Average Golfer whose main ambition is to make the ball finish somewhere on the green. Clubs of this type require a very wide sole, however, as the Sure-Out has. The Console sand wedge also creates a nice bounce effect with an extremely wide sole, but with a concave configuration.

A good sand wedge should also have a certain degree of curve from the toe to the heel of the sole, so it is higher on each end than in the middle. With the toe and the heel higher, the club is less likely to grab the sand with either end and thus turn the face inward or outward.

Among the great sand wedges I have seen are the original Wilson R-90, which appeared in the 1930's; the MacGregor sand wedges of the 1940's and 1950's, especially the latter; the 1954 model Spalding Dynamiter, and the 1973 Spalding Top-Flight. More currently, I like the 1977 and 1978 Toney Penna sand wedges, which have 9-10 degrees of inversion, about five-eighths of an inch in sole width and a nice curve from toe to heel.

Sand Play Tactics

There will never be a sand wedge that is perfect for all conditions. For one reason, the character of the sand varies greatly from course to course, sometimes from hole to hole on the same course.

Some sand is soft, porous and deep. The clubhead penetrates all too readily. To resist such penetration, you would need a sole that was extremely wide with considerable inversion.

Other sand is coarse and shallow. It resists penetration. A sole that is too inverted or too wide will bounce off the surface all too readily, often into the ball itself.

Wet sand and/or hard-packed sand similarly resist penetration and would, ideally, call for a sole that is less inverted and/or narrow.

The lie of the ball will also vary from shot to shot. When it sets atop the sand, you need a fairly shallow penetration so the clubhead doesn't cut in too far below the bottom of the ball. When the ball is buried, you need a deeper penetration to avoid skulling the shot.

Theoretically, a golfer might need to carry a dozen different types of wedges to select the one best suited for the type of sand and the particular lie he faces in a given situation. Since the rules limit the number of clubs during play to 14, carrying even two different sand wedges onto the course severely limits your overall arsenal.

Fortunately, there are ways for you to vary the depth of penetration with a single sand club. If you understand what to do to make a given club cut shallow or deep, you can use it successfully for a wide variety of sand types and ball lies.

One way is simply to vary the clubhead's angle of descent into the sand. As shown in *Illustration 30,* the more downward the clubhead is moving, the deeper it will penetrate, You can vary the club's angle of approach into the sand just as you would vary the degree that you might pinch the ball itself on a shot from grass. Again, the more you set your suspension point to the left of the ball, the steeper you can make your angle of approach.

Another way to vary your depth of cut with the same club is to vary the facing of the club. The more you turn the clubface open to the right of your target, the more you increase the inversion of its sole. Thus facing

30. Read the sand, note the lie

When the clubface is opened to the right and the clubhead's angle of approach is less steep than normal (upper illustration), the penetration of the club into the sand is minimized. Factors that require minimal penetration are also shown. Note that the ball is setting up fairly high in the sand. The sand itself is dry, porous and deep, the characteristics that can cause all too much penetration unless the club's inversion is fully utilized. The need for deeper penetration is greatest when—as shown in the lower illustration—the ball is buried and the sand is resistant, wet, hardpacked and shallow. Deeper penetration results from a steeper angle of approach and a clubface alignment—square to closed—that decreases the inversion of the club's sole.

the club to the right a bit at address limits the depth that the clubhead will enter the sand.

Conversely, the more you aim the club's facing to the left at address, the more you turn the leading edge of the sole downward. Thus a square-to-closed clubface alignment causes the leading edge to knife farther downward into the sand.

If you understand these two ways of varying the depth of cut, then all you need to do is to "read" the sand properly and note the lie of the ball beforehand. The object of reading the sand is simply to determine the extent that it will resist or encourage penetration.

Thus if you find your ball in sand near a green, you might follow this procedure:

1. Check the lie. The deeper the ball sits in the sand, the deeper the penetration must be to move the clubhead under the ball. If you see that the lie is good, with the ball setting atop or just slightly down in the sand, you would tentatively plan to play a shot with minimal clubhead penetration. In that case, you would set the clubface slightly open at address and apply my normal V-shaped swing.

If the ball is half buried, you need a deeper penetration. Thus you plan to address the shot with your sand wedge square or somewhat closed to the left and/or plan on a more upright backswing and more descending downswing. Again, lean more to the left, possibly playing the ball farther back in your stance as well to increase the angle of descent further.

If the ball is almost fully buried, I suggest you play the shot with a pitching wedge or a 9-iron. These clubs, lacking any inversion, will give you even deeper penetration. The clubhead can clear the underside of the buried ball.

2. Check the sand. After looking at the lie and deciding tentatively on the depth of cut you will need, you might want to modify your decision according to the nature of the sand itself.

If it appears that the sand is going to *resist* penetration, you will need to overcome this resistance. Thus, you should plan to create less inversion on the club by aiming it less open to the right, square or slightly

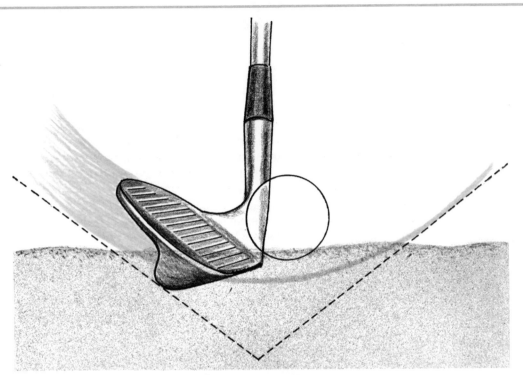

**LESS ANGLE OF APPROACH—
LESS PENETRATION**

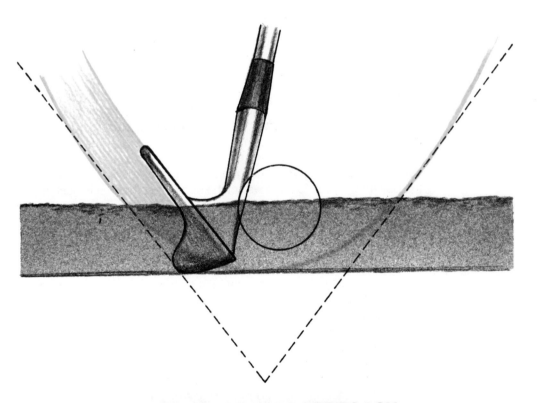

**STEEPER ANGLE OF APPROACH—
MORE PENETRATION**

closed to the left and you might also plan to create a steeper angle of approach (*refer again to Illustration 30*).

Conditions that make sand resistant to penetration are wetness, coarseness of the granules and shallowness of the depth of the sand. If I note that the sand is wet and shallow, for instance, I will certainly not play the shot in a way that may cause the clubhead to bounce off the sand and rebound upward into the ball. In fact, I may decide to discard the sand wedge altogether for fear that its wide and inverted sole might create this bouncing effect. Instead, I may well go to the pitching wedge with its downturned and sharper leading edge, just to make sure that I can slide the sole under the ball.

If the sand appears likely to *encourage* penetration, I need to play a less penetrative shot. I need to open the clubface more at address, to increase the sole's inversion and/or swing the clubhead into the sand on a shallower angle of descent.

Factors that make sand easier to penetrate are dryness, fineness of the granules and unusual depth.

You are not allowed to test the sand. You cannot touch it with your hands, for example. Nor can you touch it with your club before swinging it back to the ball. However, there are legal ways to ascertain the nature of the sand. Just walking into the bunker gives you a feeling for its depth and texture. Note how readily your feet penetrate. You can further sense the undersurface and the depth of the sand as you settle your feet into your address position. You can also notice the pattern that your ball made in the sand upon landing, before coming to rest. Did it make a deep or shallow depression when it landed? Did it bounce a bit and roll a bit thereafter? Or did it come to a quick stop and dig a fairly deep trench?

3. Decide on the shot's height and length requirements. Thus far your decision on playing the shot is still tentative, based on the lie of the ball and thereafter modified by the nature of the sand. Before making your final decision, you must decide on how high the ball must fly to clear the wall of the bunker and how far it must go to reach the hole.

Between the elements of height and length, height must be your first consideration. You must first make sure that the shot will clear the wall of the bunker. If you cannot reach the flagstick with the height of shot needed to clear the wall, so be it. It's almost always best to play the next shot from short of the hole, rather than from the same bunker you are already in.

To play a sand shot that flies high, it is best for most golfers to apply the V-shaped swing, with the clubhead moving sharply downward into the sand and with the clubface opened at least slightly to the right.

The open face adds effective loft to the club. It also keeps the club from cutting too far under the ball. Thus the abrasion created by having just a small amount of sand between the club and the ball adds backspin, and more height, to the shot. Swinging sharply downward also allows you to swing the club with added velocity without the ball flying too far. This added velocity further increases the height of the shot.

In short, to make a shot fly high, open the clubface slightly, swing steeply up and down and apply whatever velocity you need to reach the target (see *Illustration 31a*).

To make a sand shot fly far—assuming maximum height is not needed—you must create full clubhead velocity. You must also apply that force more forward, less downward. You will need to swing on a more normal, pitch-shot arc rather than on the V-shaped arc (see *Illustration 31b*).

The less-descending swing arc will increase your length on sand shots, but only to a certain extent. The sand's intervention between the club and the ball still disallows your creating anywhere near the distance you would get from grass when the clubhead made direct contact with the ball at maximum velocity.

With a bit of practice, you will discover the top distance you can expect with the normal explosion shot. When you find yourself beyond that range, you are in what I call the "gray area."

For instance, let's say you are in the sand and 30 yards from the hole. But perhaps your maximum distance on an explosion shot—even if you make a swing that is less downward than V shaped—is only, say, 20 yards. Then you have three choices:

—You could play the normal sand shot and accept the fact that you will finish short of the hole by some 10 yards.

—You could play the normal sand shot but try to contact the sand a bit closer to the ball, say, about one-half inch away. This would probably give you the extra distance you need. However, one-half inch is a dangerously small margin against error. If you should happen to catch the ball instead of the sand, you would fly it far past the target, probably over the green, because you would be swinging the club at full velocity.

—You could play a standard pitch shot, contacting the ball first and then the sand as shown in *Illustration 31c*. The main risk here is catching the sand before the ball, an all too likely possibility. Then, since you had intended to contact the ball on what amounts to a 30-yard pitch shot, you would not be swinging at anything near full velocity. If the clubhead did enter the sand beforehand, it would lack sufficient speed to make the shot carry to the target. It would finish well short of the hole. It might remain in the sand.

None of these three choices, when you are in the gray area, is ideal. Of course, when you are farther away, if you can play a normal pitch shot with a fair degree of clubhead speed, that becomes your best choice.

Other choices. Thus far I've described the basic explosion shot from sand, along with the variations to make according to the lie of the ball, the nature of the sand and the shot's height and length requirements.

31. How to control height and length

a. The high, quick-stopping sand shot results from combining maximum effective loft with a large dose of backspin. Opening the clubface at address increases its eventual effective loft. It also increases the inversion of the club's sole so the penetration will be shallow, just under the ball. The shallow penetration creates a "sandpaper" effect that increases backspin. The inversion of the sole also allows you to swing aggressively downward without cutting in too deeply. Being more aggressive adds clubhead speed which further increases the spin applied to the ball.

b. Longer sand shots require that the club's angle of approach be less steeply downward and more forward. The shallower angle of approach does increase the risk that the club will ricochet off the sand and upward into the back of the ball. This risk can be reduced, however, by squaring the clubface at address to reduce the inversion of the sole.

c. When the ball is beyond your normal sand-shot range, you will need to dispense with penetrating the sand behind the ball. Instead, merely play a normal pitch shot, making certain that your club contacts the ball before it enters the sand. You can achieve additional length by using the less-lofted pitching wedge rather than the sand wedge.

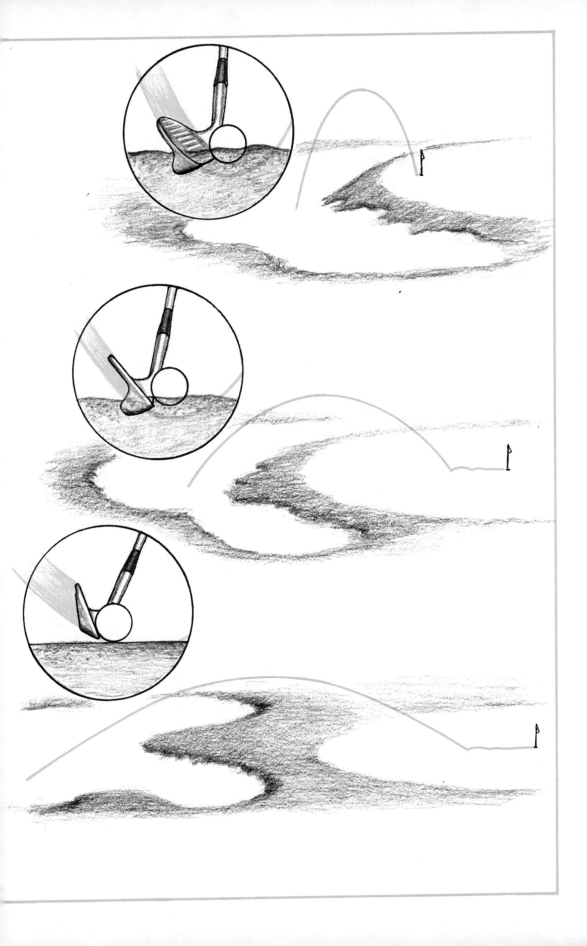

You can also putt, chip or pitch from sand. But I certainly would not advocate your using any of these methods as your basic sand technique—all are too limiting.

For instance, putting, chipping and pitching from sand all require you to contact the ball, not the sand, first. I've already explained that catching the sand first with the slower-moving clubhead that you would need on these relatively short shots all but guarantees leaving the ball short of the target, if not still in the sand.

Because the ball must be contacted first, the lie must be excellent. If the ball is even slightly buried, you will probably contact at least some sand behind it or the bare top of the ball. Again, the normal explosion shot can be applied to any type of lie.

Even from a good lie it is difficult to putt, chip or pitch if the sand is soft and fluffy. Any downward movement of the clubhead into the ball on a chip or pitch shot merely drives it deeper into the sand. The soft sand also makes it difficult to judge the amount of force needed to putt through it.

It is also difficult to get much height on even a pitch shot from sand. The downward pinching needed to avoid the sand behind the ball takes too much effective loft off the clubface.

Thus to pitch, chip or putt from a close-in bunker, you must have a good lie, firm sand and little need for height.

Given these conditions, you can putt, chip or pitch from close in. My first choice would be the putt, unless there was a lip to the bunker and/or a sizable span of grass between the bunker and the green. Then I would chip. I would not pitch the shot unless it were beyond my chip-shot range, just as I would not pitch off grass when I was within chipping distance.

Still, learning to play the normal, V-shaped explosion shot remains your best all-round sand ploy. With it, you can escape from almost any bunker situation, regardless of the ball's lie and the type of sand. Merely apply the techniques that I have mentioned after you have first considered the lie, the sand itself and the height and length of shot required. Ideally, once you master this shot, you will depart from it only when you need more distance than it can provide. Then you should play your normal pitch shot just as you would from grass, making sure that your clubhead does, in fact, contact the ball before it enters the sand.

SECTION 7: CURING SHORT-GAME PROBLEMS

Sooner or later every golfer runs into some sort of bad spell on part shots from around the green. Often, just one bad shot—a short approach that is stubbed, topped or shanked, or a short putt that is "yipped"—leads to a fear of failure and extra tension on the next similar shot. The player seems all but ordained either to repeat the error or to overcompensate and make a different bad shot. This causes more fear, more tension, more bad shots.

Some golfers understand, or at least sense, the problem. They find a cure before it becomes chronic. However, the cure itself often takes a toll. It may eliminate the disastrous shot, but it may also eventually limit the player's part-shot repertoire.

For instance, a touring professional once came to me for a pitching lesson. As it turned out, his case history had gone like this.

Originally he had been bothered by sometimes stubbing his clubhead into the ground behind the ball.

To eliminate this "fat" shot, he had unconsciously begun to slide his suspension point at the nape of his neck to the left during the down-swing. Thus he was severely pinching his pitch shots. This greatly reduced his club's effective loft at impact. The ball flew too low and bounded too far forward on the green before its backspin could make it grab the putting surface.

He had solved one problem—the stubbing—but in doing so he had lost the high, soft pitch shot he needed when he was playing to a limited landing area. He had reduced his part-shot repertoire. Whenever he did try to play the high, soft shot by lessening the amount he pinched the ball, he once again ran the risk of stubbing.

For me to help this pupil play this shot without fear of stubbing, I had to help him eliminate the cause of the stubbing. This was not difficult. And it was worth the price of admission to see his shots float high in the air and settle on the green like a duck landing on water.

I will tell you what I explained and prescribed to this professional, because the things I pointed out apply to all who stub, or top, shots.

Stubbing And Topping

Yes, stubbing and topping are closely allied, even though the shots look and feel vastly different. Topping is often an overreaction to stubbing, and vice-versa. Also, as I told my pupil, while both stubbing and topping can result from many different causes, there is one overall principle that applies in every case. I call this the "radius principle."

This principle involves two distances, both of which are measured from the left shoulder. One is the distance from it to the bottom of the ball. The other is the distance from that shoulder to the bottom of the clubhead. This latter distance can be loosely described as the radius of the swing.

If these two distances are practically identical at impact, you will neither stub nor top the shot. You will stub it if the distance from the shoulder to the bottom of the club—the radius—is greater than the distance from the shoulder to the bottom of the ball. You will top the shot if the radius is more than just fractionally shorter than the distance to the bottom of the ball.

I once asked a mathematician in the space program how far I would hit behind the ball if my radius were seven feet in length and *one inch longer* than the distance from the shoulder to the bottom of the ball. He said I would catch the ground about 18 inches behind the ball. If my radius were six feet and I misjudged by that same one inch, the contact would be about 15 inches back of the ball. Obviously, solid contact involves a large degree of precision.

This need for precision becomes even more ominous when you consider these facts:

1. Since the left shoulder does move during the swing, its distance from the bottom of the ball is always changing.

2. Since the wrists cock and uncock during the swing, the distance from the shoulder to the bottom of the club also changes. It shortens during the backswing as the wrists cock; it lengthens during the downswing as they uncock.

3. During the downswing primarily, the weight of the moving clubhead creates a pulling force on the hands and arms. This pulling force—centrifugal force—makes your wrists and arms want to

straighten. This also increases the length of your radius, the distance from your shoulder to the bottom of the club.

The reason why my pupil stubbed his shots was because he failed to allow for this straightening beforehand when he addressed the shot. He set up with his hands too low. This created a large break at the wrists, which centrifugal force straightened during his downswing. Thus, his radius at impact was longer than it had been at address, so he stubbed his shots.

He could have solved the problem from the start by just gripping farther down on the club. This would have extended his left arm and left wrist at address to more or less the same degree they were extended at impact. In fact, this was the correction I prescribed that eventually eliminated the stubbing (*see Illustration 32*).

My pupil had found a way to eliminate the stubbing on his own, but it was a compensatory action. It failed to deal with the original problem, the low setting of his hands at address and the break in the radius that this created.

His compensation—again, to move well ahead of the ball during his downswing—moved his left shoulder farther from the ball at impact than it had been at address. The increased distance from shoulder to ball provided enough clearance for the increased radius that occurred during his downswing, when the weight of the moving club straightened his wrists and arms. However, as I said, moving ahead of the ball made him pinch the shot too severely and made his shots fly too low.

Another golfer might have found a different way to compensate or provide clearance for the swing radius. Lifting up—raising the suspension point during the swing—would be one way. Another would be to flinch, to pull up just the arms as they swung into the ball.

In either case, the player would probably avoid stubbing. However, if he lifted or flinched too much, he would top the shot.

There are many other causes of stubbing and topping other than setting the hands too low at address. Again, all create some degree of difference between the distance from the left shoulder to the bottom of the ball and the distance from that shoulder to the bottom of the club itself at impact.

Generally, too much bending or crouching at address will force you to lift your suspension point during the downswing or flinch and lift your arms.

Sliding your suspension point to the left during your downswing can make you top shots. Since the left shoulder thus moves farther from the ball, your radius cannot reach the full distance to the bottom of the ball.

If you slide your suspension point to the right, you may either stub the club into the ground behind the ball, or you may top the ball with the clubhead already moving upward (*see Illustration 32*).

Poor timing can also cause stubbing or topping. If your arms swing

32. Topping, stubbing cures

a. The left arm and the clubshaft form a radius in the golf swing. Stubbed shots occur when this radius is longer than the distance from the left shoulder to the bottom of the ball at contact. Topped shots occur when the radius is too short. The upper drawings show the importance of maintaining a steady suspension point during the swing. Sliding it to the left increases the distance from the shoulder to the ball beyond the length of the left arm-clubshaft radius, so topping occurs. Sliding it back to the right causes stubbing with the ground behind the ball or topping because of contact occurring on the upswing.

b. The sideviews on the right show proper address positioning, with the hands set low on the clubshaft so the left arm can be extended, as contrasted with too much arm bend at address and too much knee flex. The latter position brings the left shoulder too close to the ball so the normal extending of the left arm and wrists that occurs during the swing creates stubbing. Stubbing, in turn, may make the golfer react by lifting his arms or his suspension point during the swing and, as a result, he may actually top future shots.

a.

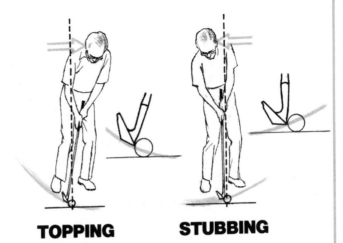

TOPPING   **STUBBING**

YES

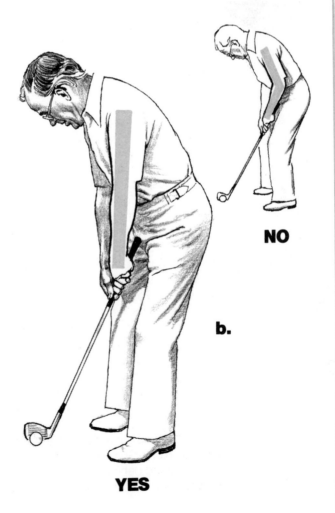

NO

b.

YES

down too soon, you will tend to stub the shot. This happens because the early straightening of the arms and wrists increases the length of the radius before the left shoulder has had sufficient time to swing upward and turn to the left to provide enough clearance between it and the bottom of the ball.

Conversely, if you are late with your arms and the uncocking of your wrists, you will tend to top the shot. By the time your radius is finally extended fully, your left shoulder has already turned and lifted so far that the distance from it to the bottom of the ball is longer than the radius.

Checklist. If you tend to top or stub your shots, check to make sure that:

1. You are addressing the ball with enough left-arm extension, as shown in *Illustration 32*. As you set up to the shot, anticipate and duplicate the extension of this arm that you will have at impact. To get this left-arm extension at address, grip well down on the clubshaft. If you were to grip near the top of the club and extend your left arm, you would be forced to stand too tall or too far from the ball. In either case, you would be too far from your work to make solid contact consistently. Also, you would be forced to swing on a plane that is too flat.

2. You are addressing the ball and not the ground behind it. So make sure your clubhead sets very lightly on the grass behind the ball, not with its full weight on the ground.

3. You are flexed only slightly at the knees. You should be bending forward from the hips to swing on an upright plane. Too much knee flex may cause you to lift your suspension point or flinch with your arms to avoid stubbing.

4. Your weight is more or less evenly distributed between your feet. This will set your suspension point in a more or less neutral spot so it will not slide dramatically to the left or right as you swing. The exceptions to this rule would apply only on longer pitch shots that you wish to lob or on short pitches you wish to pinch quite severely. To lob a longer pitch with a level-moving clubhead at impact, set your suspension point a bit more to the right. To pinch a short pitch with a downward moving clubhead, set it more to the left. Unless you are a good golfer, however, it is risky to set your weight to the right on short pitch shots or too far to the left on long pitches.

5. You are swinging with your suspension point staying in position. Though few golfers can actually hold it perfectly steady from takeaway through impact, that should be your goal. If this point at the nape of your neck is higher or lower at impact than it was at address, you run the risk of topping or stubbing, respectively.

If it moves out of position to the right, you will reach your full extension of radius *before* the clubhead gets to the ball. It will either stub in the ground behind the ball or arrive at the ball already swinging upward, so you either skull, or top, the shot.

Sliding the suspension point to the left will cause your full extension of the radius to occur too late, *after* the clubhead has already reached the ball. In a sense, this is a lesser evil than shifting your suspension point to the right in that your bad shot will always be topped, not stubbed or topped. Also, the clubhead will be moving downward at impact, not upward. Thus, if you should happen to catch the ball slightly below its equator, you will apply enough backspin to get at least some height on the shot and some stopping action on the green. Again, however, swinging with little or no suspension-point movement is the ideal.

Shanking

The shank is the worst shot in golf. It has no redeeming virtue.

The slice can be useful for curving the ball around obstacles. So can the hook. The controlled slice—the fade—increases height and spin to make the shot settle quickly on the green. The controlled hook—the draw—adds distance because of its lesser amount of backspin. The pull to the left and the push to the right, while unfortunate, at least go a long way because the contact is solid. The controlled stub—the "explosion" shot—is useful, not only from sand, but from tight lies on turf or bare ground when the situation demands a high trajectory. Even the purposely topped shot is being used by more and more expert golfers on short run-up shots to make the ball walk forward through the grass around the greens.

But a shank is a shank. It is golf's Black Death.

It cannot be controlled because the ball is struck with the rounded hosel of the iron, where the shaft enters the head. It spurts off somewhere, anywhere, to the right, low and hard.

It feeds on itself. The tension it generates—rigidity in the wrists and arms—shortens backswings and impairs squaring of the clubface, both of which can cause more shanking.

It happens most frequently on the costly short approach shots, where the backswing is relatively short anyway.

And shanking can strike any golfer without warning. It is only a slight generalization to say that, surprisingly, the better player is somewhat more susceptible.

This is true because of the nature of the shank itself. For a shot to be shanked, one or both of two things must happen. Less commonly, the clubface might be so open at contact, facing so far to the right, that the hosel leads the rest of the clubhead into the ball by a wide margin. More frequently, the clubhead will be shoved outward from far inside the target line, leaving only the hosel for contact. In that instance we usually have a combination of the two—the clubhead moving out beyond the ball with the face open as well.

More good golfers have already mastered the correct clubhead path, that being from inside to along the target line, than have poorer players who more often swing from out to in. Thus the path normal for the good player is more akin to the inside-to-outside path that leads to shanking that the out-to-in path used by most higher handicap golfers.

To cure shanking, I suggest you focus your efforts on eliminating the shoving of the clubhead out beyond the ball. Not only is this a more common cause of shanking than the exceedingly open clubface, but, moreover, some of the things I will suggest to eliminate this outward shoving will also reduce or eliminate the open face.

Start by looking at *Illustration 33*. Here we show a golfer at address with a line drawn from the ball up through the suspension point at the nape of his neck.

In the illustration, we see the golfer near the top of the backswing with the left arm swinging on three planes. One of these arm planes is more upright than the plane from the ball through the suspension point. One is identical. One is flatter or below the suspension-point plane.

From studying this illustration it should be apparent that swinging the arm on the flatter plane is most likely to channel the clubhead outward beyond the ball, causing a shank.

The most upright arm plane is more likely to swing the club more downward and less outward. This plane is least likely to cause a shank, though it might lead to the opposite effect, which would be to contact the ball out toward the toe of the club.

If you are in the throes of shanking, however, this anti-shank arm plane would be best for swinging the club more downward and less outward beyond the ball.

Many golfers arrive at this more upright arm plane by starting the backswing to the inside on a flat plane, with the arm moving well around to the inside. Thereafter, they swing it upward and outward to the upright plane. Because from there the club moves more downward and less outward, they do not tend to shank their long shots. However, on short shots, where the backswing is short, they do not have sufficient time to move from flat to upright. Thus it is not a good idea to swing the club abruptly to the inside during the takeaway, especially on short shots.

In *Illustration 33* we also see three different positions formed by the back of the left wrist. We show the wrist bowed (convex), straight (the so-called "square" position) and cupped (concave). You will notice how the position of the wrist affects the plane of the clubshaft. In each instance, the plane of the shaft is flatter when the wrist is bowed than when it is square. The shaft is most upright when the wrist is cupped or concave.

Again, the flatter plane is more likely to channel the clubhead outward beyond the ball and cause a shank. The more upright plane is more likely to channel it downward and less outward, more on an anti-shank path.

Thus the square-wrist position is better than the bowed, or convex,

33. Shanking—cause and cure

a. On normal non-cut shots, as shown at right, the club is swung on a plane that more or less conforms to a line extending upward from the ball and through the suspension point. At the top of the backswing, the left wrist is cupped inward slightly. Contact occurs near the center of the clubface.

b. The dreaded shank is shown in the middle of these three sets of illustrations. The swing is relatively flat in comparison with the more upright line formed between the ball and the suspension point at the base of the neck (dashed line). Also, the back of the left wrist has been bowed outward. Thus the club finishes the backswing moving and pointing backward behind the golfer. The downswing becomes, in reaction, an outward shoving. The clubhead moves out beyond the ball so contact occurs on the hosel.

c. The bottom illustrations show the anti-shank swing. The golfer swings the club on a plane that is more upright than the norm, with the back of the left wrist cupping well inward. If the hands and arms remain free of tension, the clubhead swings into the ball from outside-to-inside the line, with contact tending to occur toward the toe of the clubface. As the player gains confidence, he can digress from the anti-shank swing to the normal swing.

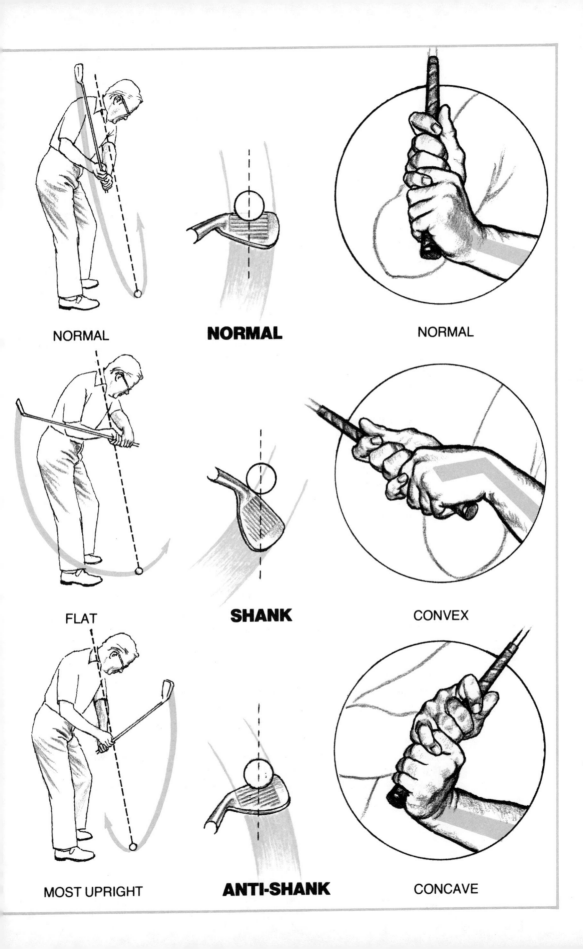

NORMAL

NORMAL

NORMAL

FLAT

SHANK

CONVEX

MOST UPRIGHT

ANTI-SHANK

CONCAVE

position, and the cupped, or concave, wrist position is better than either, if your goal is to end shanking.

The position of your wrist at the top of the swing depends a great deal on how you start your backswing. If you start the clubhead back fractionally *before* you move your left arm, you will tend to move into, or at least toward, the bowed-wrist position. If you make a one-piece takeaway, in which the clubhead and left arm move in *unison,* you will tend neither to bow nor cup your wrist any more than it was at address. If you start your left arm back a fraction before your clubhead retreats from the ball, you will tend to swing into the cupped-wrist—the anti-shank—position.

To swing this way, I suggest you hold the club lightly in your hands at address and throughout your swing. Your wrists and arms should feel light and flexible. Too much tension, the normal result of shanking, creates the short, flat backswing that creates the outward-moving, shank-producing clubhead path on the downswing.

Checklist.   Your anti-shank technique should include:

—Light grip pressure at address and throughout your swing.

—Starting the left arm back slightly in advance of the clubhead, to reach the slightly cupped wrist position.

—Swinging the left arm up and down on an upright plane.

A good way to simulate these three points is merely to address the ball with a light grip and then:

—Without straightening up, cock your wrists upward and raise your hands to the side of your right cheek.

—Make your full backswing turn.

—Hit the shot.

If what I've said so far does not cure your shanking, please make sure that your feet and body are aligned parallel to your target line at address. If you have been aligning too far to the left, your right side may be getting in the way of your arms during your downswing, forcing the club outward beyond the ball. If you have been aligning your feet or your body too far to the right, your left side may be blocking the way of your arms and causing a similar outward movement of the club.

Finally, in a few instances I have seen players who do everything I've said and still shove the club outward with their arms during the downswing. In these cases, I have found it helpful for them to imagine a pole stuck in the ground, just fractionally on the ball side of where their hands are at address. They solve their shanking problem by merely swinging their arms through the impact area without the hands bumping into the "pole."

Missing Short Putts

Shortly before World War II, I had two pupils who were utterly spastic on short putts. Their nervous systems could not cope with these seemingly simple tries they knew they were supposed to sink.

To solve their problem so they could continue to enjoy their golf, I devised for them what I call the "split-hand" style of putting. I reasoned that anyone who failed with a conventional putting method might well succeed with an unconventional method, which split-hand putting certainly is. It worked.

Split-hand putting allows you to stroke the ball solidly in the right direction, even when you feel as if you are about to lose your lunch. Split-hand putting is a must for people who become too emotionally involved on short putts.

I do not advise the split-hand style for long putts, however. Distance becomes too difficult to control. For most people, 8 to 10 feet is the outer limit, except when the greens are lightning-fast or if the putt is extremely downhill.

I use the split-hand method myself, but not because of any problem with my nerves. I merely feel that it is a more efficient technique on short putts. I think it saves me about one shot per round on average. However, if the putt is so long that I must debate between using the split-hand or conventional technique, I will always go with the conventional.

Illustration 34 shows me addressing and stroking a putt split-handed. Notice that in some respects my positions are identical to those I advocate for conventional putting. You should be sure to assume these same positions when using the split-hand technique. Particularly, my feet point straight forward, at right angles to my putting line. Neither is closer to that line than the other. My eyes are directly over the line. The shaft of the putter is vertical, tilted neither to the left nor the right. My weight is evenly distributed between my two feet. The putter is aimed directly down the putting line.

The departures in positioning you should notice and apply are:

1. The top of the putter sets firmly against the stomach, about an inch or an inch and a half to the left of its center.

2. The left forearm anchors tightly against—actually it is buried

into—the stomach, just left of center.

3. The left hand clenches—yes, clenches—the putter with a viselike grip.

4. The right hand rests lightly against the back of the puttershaft well below its middle. The forefinger extends downward. It sets against the putter as lightly as the left hand clenches it tightly. The right hand is the propelling hand, the left the holding hand.

5. The right arm is almost fully extended. Actually, you should first extend it fully and then slide the hand up the shaft an inch or two, just enough to eliminate any tension in that arm.

6. The feet are spread extremely far apart. The exact width of stance will depend largely on the length of your putter and your legs. You should spread them far enough apart, however, so that your eyes do set directly over the putting line.

This is not a comfortable address position by any means, especially when you first try it, and especially if you clench the putter with your left hand as tightly as you should. What's a little discomfort compared to the anguish of missing a two-foot putt?

The stroke itself should be made solely with the right arm moving back and forward rhythmically. It accelerates the putterhead into the ball smoothly. The left hand merely holds on, with the left arm remaining immobile against your stomach. The left wrist hinges slightly, but only as a reaction to the movement of the putter, just as a gate hinges when it is opened and closed.

If you do not let the top of the putter move back and forward one iota, and if you hold the club very lightly in your right hand with absolutely no increase in grip pressure, the putterhead will swing in its proper path. It will return to its original facing.

When you first try this method, you may find that your putterhead does not move on the same path every time. This probably indicates that you need (1) a firmer anchoring of your left forearm against your stomach, (2) an adjustment of your right-hand grip—be sure this palm and extended forefinger rest against the back of the shaft facing down the line, (3) a lighter right-hand grip pressure that never increases during the stroke, (4) a more rhythmical stroke, (5) a wider stance or (6) to address the putt with the putterhead setting lightly on the grass—do not push it downward.

Check these things and the other positions I have mentioned. Within one or two brief practice sessions you will begin to make a consistent stroke. You will find that your confidence on short putts increases, not only because the method itself is so reliable, but because it positions your head so much closer to the ball and the putting line. You may find this intimacy with your work makes these short putts actually look much simpler to you than they ever have before.

34. Split-hand putting

Here we see the proper positioning and stroking for split-hand putting, described in this chapter. This highly reliable method is recommended only for short putts, within 8 to 10 feet, except when the green is exceptionally fast or the putt is downhill. The method is especially beneficial for golfers who cannot cope with nervousness on these putts.

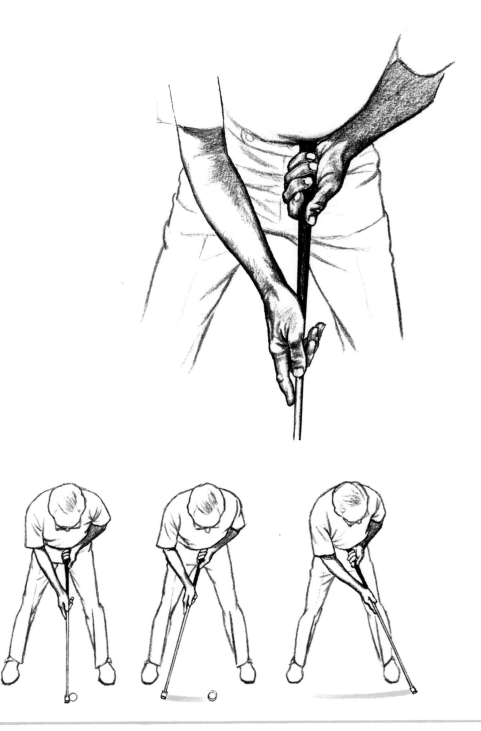

SECTION 8: PROFITABLE PRACTICE

I would like you to estimate two things about your golf game:

—If you added together all the putts, chips, pitches and sand shots you take during an average round of golf, what percentage would that total represent of your overall score?

—What percentage of your total practice time do you devote to these shots?

I strongly suspect that your answer to the first question will be at least 50 percent, probably quite higher. I doubt that your second answer will be nearly as high.

If my suspicions are valid, you are seriously limiting yourself at golf, not scoring nearly as well as you could.

If, say, 65 percent of the strokes you take on the course are short-game shots, then you should be devoting 65 percent of your practice time to them.

I think this makes sense, especially when you consider that:

1. You do not need to drive to the range to work on many of your part shots. The living room carpet or the back yard will suffice for a short session perhaps before dinner.

2. Working on your short game is the quickest way to lower your scores. It can happen overnight.

3. Some progress is all but guaranteed.

4. It doesn't cost anything—no range fees.

5. Short-game practice, as we shall see, can be great fun.

When and what to practice. I strongly advocate regular practice sessions rather than the occasional, extended session. A half-hour or an hour each day or every other day is far better than two to four hours all at once every other week.

I say this because one goal of short-game practice is not only to *maintain* a fine sense of touch, but also gradually to *heighten* that sense. You want your engine to purr all the time, but if it purrs like a well-tuned compact car in May or June, you should want it to purr like a perfectly instrumented Cadillac or Rolls-Royce in August or September. While occasional practice is better than no practice, you will probably find yourself spending most of that session merely warming up your engine to purr at all.

Also, since part shots require more sensitivity than do full-swing shots, practicing them properly demands more concentration on each and every stroke. The eventual loss of concentration that will occur during a longer session—say midway through—makes the rest of that session a waste of your time.

The amount of time within a given session that you devote to each aspect of the short game should depend, naturally, on the part or parts you think need the most work. However, there are some general points to remember.

Putting and chipping practice is more debilitating than pitching or sand practice. The constant crouching involved on those shots will quickly stiffen your back, for instance. During a general short-game practice session, I would work on my pitch or sand shots between the times that I worked on my putts and chip shots. I might also work for a longer period on the pitches, not only because they are less demanding physically, but also because—as I have stressed—they are more difficult to play well.

I strongly advise that before a round of play you practice your putting and chipping *before* you warm up with your pitch shots and full swings. Reversing this order is bad business because, again, putting and chipping tie your muscles into knots, which is not what you want on that first tee shot.

Inward practice vs. outward practice. There are really two distinct reasons for practicing. One is to improve your technique, your mechanics; the other, to translate your improved technique into better results.

It is best that you do not confuse these two goals during your practice sessions. You will not do a very good job of improving your technique if you become overly concerned about the results of your shots. You will not get good results if you are thinking about your technique as you swing.

Developing your mechanics requires *inward* thinking, focusing solely on yourself, your address position and your swinging of the club.

Translating improved technique into better results requires *outward* thinking, focusing on your target and the shot—how high it will fly, where it will land, how far it will run—both before and during your stroke.

Take putting, for instance. If better technique is my goal, if I'm trying to grip the club and set up to the ball and make my stroke the same way every time, I would not putt to a hole. I would have my balls close at hand so I could drag one into the exact same position every time without ever moving my feet. I might even put a coin down on the green in front of me to be sure I'd place every ball in the same place—just to my side of the coin—on every putt. I probably would not even look up to note where each putt finished. My total focus would be inward, on making my mechanics consistently correct every time.

Thereafter, to translate my improved mechanics into successful results, I would putt to a hole. I would continue to putt from the same spot, still without changing my address position between putts, but my focus would be solely on sinking the putt. I would be thinking about the target, not my stroke, every time.

This same separation of thinking, inward vs. outward, applies to all part shots, in fact, to your full-swing practice as well. Never worry about your shots when you are practicing your mechanics; and never think about your mechanics when you are practicing your shots.

Practice the way you play. The final goal of practice is to improve your shots on the course. Therefore, your final step in practicing—putts, chips or whatever—is to perform in ways that closely simulate actual playing conditions.

To practice chip and pitch shots as you will encounter them on the course, you should scatter your balls at random in different places around the green. You should play each ball from whatever lie it happens to finish in.

You should do the same pre-shot planning for each of these shots that you would use on the course. Initially, you should let the lie determine whether you will lob, slightly pinch or severely pinch the shot. You should decide on the trajectory you will need to make the ball land on the green and finish near the hole with a shot of minimum air length and maximum ground length. You should choose the club you think will provide that trajectory when struck with the degree of pinch, if any, you feel you need. You should finally decide whether you can chip the ball to your landing spot with that club, or whether you will need to pitch it.

Your address routine on each practice shot should also be the same as it is on the course. If, for instance, you waggle the club three times on the course, you should waggle it three times on each practice shot.

All of these things breed consistency of stroke and shot results. They also increase your confidence so that varying situations on the course do not seem quite so foreign.

On the putting green, once you've developed your mechanics, you should vary your putts just as they will be varied on the course. You might, for instance, putt just one ball to each of the various holes. If you have a 9-hole putting clock on your practice green, you might first play the holes in order, then reverse order. Thereafter, you might putt to the odd-numbered holes and then the even-numbered holes, then backward to the even-numbered holes followed by the odd-numbered ones. On each putt you should read the green, make your practice stroke(s) and address the putt the same way you do on the course.

Compete with yourself. No matter what you are practicing, there is almost always some way to compete against yourself. Create a challenge and try to meet it. This makes practice fun. It also simulates another aspect of on-course play—it teaches you to perform under pressure.

For example, if I'm practicing my pitch shots, I might scatter 50 balls around the practice green at various spots that are within 100 yards of the hole, but still out beyond my chipping range.

I challenge myself to make each of these shots land on the green and still finish on the green. If all 50 land on and finish on the green, I win. If one lands short, which is the likeliest danger, or if one rolls over the green, I lose. Then I must retrieve the balls I've played and start all over.

I can assure you that by the time I've played, say, 44 or 45 shots successfully, the pressure really begins to build on those that remain.

If I'm practicing my short chip shots from just off the edge of the green, I give myself a different challenge. Then my goal is to chip and putt out those 50 balls in less than 100 strokes, or under a two-stroke-per-ball average. If my total is under 100, I win. If it's over 100, I lose and must repeat the whole thing.

If I'm practicing putting, I may try to "play" 18 holes in less than 30 putts. Or I may play 18 holes with two balls. Then my goal might be to total less than 30 putts with the first ball I putt on each hole and under 28 with the second.

I frequently practice putting solely for proper distance, as you should do also . Here I might put a coin on the green just one putter-length from the fringe. I'd scatter the balls at random elsewhere on the green and then putt to the coin. My challenge would be to make at least four of every five balls finish short of the fringe, yet either level with or beyond the coin.

I especially like this challenge because the balls finish so close together that they are easy to gather up.

Obviously, you don't need 50 balls to create a challenge for yourself. And the severity of the challenge you set will vary depending on your current skill level.

You may find it sufficiently challenging, for instance, to land and stop only 50 percent of your pitch shots on the green, or to chip and hole out in an average of three strokes per ball, or to putt 18 holes in a total of, say, 36 strokes.

An additional benefit of competitive practice is that it allows you to measure your progress readily from week to week in a given area of the short game. As your skill improves in that area, you can gradually challenge yourself more severely.

And, meeting and overcoming a challenge is actually what this book is all about. I have challenged you to apply your mind and body toward improving your short game. I hope you will accept my challenge and use the tools I have supplied to meet it. In the end, I hope you will reap the universal satisfaction that goes with improving yourself, no matter what the endeavor may be.